REVELATION:

THE PROPHECY AND FULFILLMENT OF MAN

by George Denninger

Published by PublishingGood.com
U.S.A.

Publishing Good
Saint Louis, MO
www.PublishingGood.com

First Edition

ISBN 978-0-9848406-0-1 (pbk)

Library of Congress Control Number: 2012902957

Printed and bound in the United States of America

Cover design and layout by the author

Table of Contents

Preface

If I knocked on your door and heralded with great joy, 'Messias has returned; come and see,' would you jump up and prepare to follow me, would you be curious, or would you think I was mad? If I told you that the appearance and confirmation of the promised Comforter is documented in a book that was written almost two thousand years ago, would you settle back in your seat, suspect I was trying to deceive you, turn away, and go back to what you were doing? Christian and Jew alike are waiting for someone to come and save them from the prison of ignorance, and all this time the door has been unlocked!

Jesus promised his disciples in his day, "This generation shall not pass away, till all be fulfilled" (Luke 21:32). This book explores the best evidence we have that Jesus kept his promise when he delivered the Comforter to all mankind in St. John's book of *Revelation*.

True to historic precedent, the answers are neither the handout nor the form that we expected.

> And when he was demanded of the Pharisees, when the kingdom of God should come, he answered them and said, The kingdom of God cometh not with observation: Neither shall they say, Lo here! or, lo there! for, behold, the kingdom of God is within you (Luke 17:20–21).

John waited expectantly for sixty years to realize the substance of these statements, confirming Jesus' provocative comment to Peter about him: "If I will that he tarry till I come, what is that to thee? follow thou me" (John 21:22). According to several records, John's enemies did everything they could think of to destroy him, including lowering him into a pot of boiling oil, but he turned every attack into a blessing. Instead of dying as they expected, he was invigorated by the ordeal. Never giving in to malice, witnesses said they could hear him singing hymns amidst the flames. John's reputation grew so powerfully that the news could not be contained, so he was removed to the island of Patmos, which was a rock-quarry prison. Through his harassment, defamation of character, attempted murder, and confinement, he rejoiced. He said that he was on Patmos "for the word of God and for the testimony of Jesus Christ." It was there that he received and faithfully recorded the unveiling of Jesus Christ.

Was this John's reward for such faithful service, that he would be the first to document the appearance of the Comforter? Is it possible that his preparation and revelation represent a pattern that must repeat itself in every individual who hungers and thirsts after righteousness? If so, it is a universal phenomenon and one worth pondering.

> So Christ was once offered to bear the sins of many; and unto them that look for him shall he appear the second time without sin unto salvation (Heb 9:28).

If the Children of Israel, four hundred years enslaved in Egypt, had known in advance the pathway out of their own depravity, perhaps they would not have taken so long to achieve that objective. If Christians today know the end from the beginning, perhaps they will strive more vigorously to follow Jesus in *the way*: healing the sick, rousing the dead, cleansing contagion, and casting out devils. Christ promised that 'I' will come to you—the 'I,' Christ, will reveal all things to you. Six decades after his ascension, Jesus' presence returned to John. Are we dismayed because the description of that vision is not easily apprehended? Do we read it once, close the book and walk away, waiting for our ignorance to be forgiven? Jesus demanded us to work it out, not wait it out! Revelation is written in Spirit language and requires spiritual insight to be understood. Revelation is the unveiling of Life, Truth, and Love that dawns on each one of us as we realize our proper place and identity as sons and daughters of God.

SCRIPTURAL EVOLUTION

Scripture traces the evolution of man's spiritual quest to find reality. Like artists painting grand scenes, the prophets translated holy visions into physical symbols and written metaphors, which gradually became clearer and more detailed as the truth of being was better understood. Abraham built an altar on a mountaintop and prepared it for human sacrifice to illustrate his conviction that God is Father. Noah built an ark to preserve life. Jacob built a rock pillar as a reminder that God was there. Moses built a temple in the wilderness, where the holy of holies and the ark of the testimony presented assurance of the Mind of God. Mary conceived the idea of man as Messiah and brought forth Jesus, the highest symbol of Godlikeness appreciable to humanity. Jesus offered evidence of man's divine nature and immortality by his resurrection and ascension. At the conclusion of the New Testament, Jesus' revelation presents the supreme example of spiritual insight as the Bible reveals it.

The apostle John was the first to record Jesus' fulfillment of his own prophecy, which includes a description of man's journey from ignorance and sin to the sublime awareness of New Jerusalem and the cessation of time. Once we begin to see the holy purpose behind the symbols, we can reflect back and see how poignantly accurate were the primitive depictions. For example, Moses' temple can be seen as a symbol of man's perception of himself: fleshy, ignorant, and opaque if viewed from the outside with physical eyes, or wholly inspired consciousness if viewed from the inside as the center of divine intelligence.

THE TRUE COMFORTER

> No prophecy of the scripture is of any private interpretation (2 Pet. 1:20).

Being "in the Spirit on the Lord's day," turning and seeing it for oneself as John did on Patmos, is the only way to receive the true interpretation of Scripture. From this standpoint, translating the symbols back to their original spiritual language is easy. To achieve that ultimate objective, we must begin with a meek and contrite heart, looking away from a physical sense of earth and man, standing mentally still like Moses at the Red Sea. We must be willing to give up all—everything of this world—in order to gain the peace, joy, and life we are seeking. The book of Revelation assures us that there is no question of our redemption; we have no choice, for we are the manifestation of God now. What it takes for us to realize this fact is symbolized in St. John's book. We will either turn and behold *the truth of being* or we will experience all the plagues written in this book until we are forced to admit *the truth of being.* As we discover the key and begin to unlock its secrets, the Revelation of Jesus Christ becomes an open book.

> And I saw the dead, small and great, stand before God; and the books were opened (Rev. 20:12).

LITERAL INTERPRETATIONS

For centuries prior to Jesus' arrival, the Jews were expecting a messiah: one who would come and fight their immediate enemies and restore Jerusalem and the Promised Land politically and beneficially back to them exclusively. Very few people in Jesus' day recognized him as the Messiah or the Christ because he was not what they were expecting. Because of man's craving for physical solutions rather than spiritual peace, he is still trying to petition God to intervene in the affairs of this world. This common propensity seeks a literal interpretation of Revelation, attempting to associate the accompanying symbols with historic places, times, and people.

There is not a shred of evidence that Jesus concerned himself with such things as who governed Rome or who owned what piece of land. The great exemplar owned nothing, sought no political or religious office, and held none. Why would he, sixty years after his ascension, be concerned with man's affairs? Here on earth, he played the part of an elder: serving the needs of the local people by transforming them from within, teaching them to love impartially, and encouraging them to leave all and follow in *the way*. Should not we suspect that his revelation would continue preparing the hearts of his students with higher and more spiritual lessons?

> I am he which searcheth the reins and hearts (Rev. 2:23).

Revelation is presented to us as a Christ helpmeet. Attracting and gathering lost sheep requires two strategies: first, we are drawn by the sweetness and comfort of the message; and second, we are bridled to keep us from our propensities (wicked inclinations) until we learn to live by grace alone and to love it. The great Teacher taught both the beauty of holiness and the wretchedness of evil. He "loved righteousness, and hated iniquity" (Heb. 1:9).

Do not be discouraged if you do not comprehend the full meaning of the book of Revelation at your first perusal. You must know the end from the beginning, so read through to the end and then begin again. We all must discover that Revelation describes the unveiling of one's real self.

THE NATURE OF REVELATORY WRITING

If you were to think of the book of Revelation as written on a transparent sphere and you were to scan it from side to side, you would see a horizon on one side, a middle section, and a horizon on the other side. It might appear to have a beginning, middle, and end, but if you were to look again at the sphere from a different vantage point, a new beginning, a new middle, and a new end would appear; the message would be the same and yet new because of the way you were looking at it. The prophetic writing style is unique in that you can open such a document at random, start at almost any sentence, and begin reading. In Revelation, every passage contains a gene of Truth that could, if heeded and followed to its logical conclusion, regenerate the rest of the book. Needless to say, this rare type of prophetic writing is replete with meaning and needs to be thoughtfully and thoroughly studied.

Now, if you think of this sphere as if it were woven with concentric threads, it would be possible to follow one thread, or idea, all the way around the sphere, learning as you go, and arrive back where you started. If you were to start again, following around the sphere and retaining what you learned, new meanings would arise that were not apparent before. When you were satisfied, you might select another thread of truth to follow, and so on. This ascending pathway of divine wisdom and its attending grace is the nature of the human pursuit of revelation until the time when it is delivered to you directly and instantaneously, as it was to John.

PATTERN WITH A PURPOSE

Revelation is not written like a novel designed with a surprise or mysterious climax. The end is clearly stated at the beginning, even though we may not recognize it at first. To prepare our thought for each spiritual lesson, prophetic reminders are offered along the way. Like a scientific investigation, each vision magnifies the previous one, as though we were repeatedly peering through a microscope with ever more powerful lenses until the mystery of evil is uncovered and man's true identity is revealed.

Revelation is divided into an introduction, seven letters to seven churches, seven visions, a conclusion, and a recapitulation. Symbols abound, including mathematical prowess. For example, seven is a prime number and stands for indivisibility. The sequence from one through seven is also significant, and the seven days of creation in Genesis sets the standard. Each primary element builds upon the previous one, as if colors were being added to a rainbow or instruments to an orchestra. The sixth message, event, or vision is a climax, key, or compound concept, which inevitably brings on an epoch change, or a grand mental chemicalization. The seventh in the sequence presents the solution or a new state of being and wholeness or a mirror opposite of these.

In the first chapter of Genesis, creation begins with light and gradually develops over six days into higher forms of goodness until the highest state—man, made in the image and likeness of God—is seen and acknowledged. "And on the seventh day God ended his work which he had made; and he rested on the seventh day " (Gen. 2: 2).

It is most significant that the first record of creation in Genesis presents the universe from God's point of view.

> And God saw every thing that he had made, and, behold, it was very good (Gen. 1:31).

Therefore, man who is made as image and likeness of the divine 'I,' or Us, is a God-projected man.

Beginning in Genesis 2:4, a second and distinctly different record presents creation as an inverted image of the first. Here, man is created at the beginning and is made of dust from beneath rather than light from above. In this usage, Lord God, Jehovah, is God from man's vantage point: a composite of beliefs and conclusions drawn from the experiences of the Jewish nation. This is a man-projected God knowing good and evil.

Revelation restores creation to its original record, exchanging man's view of God for God's view of man. Is this not the Comforter bringing all things to our remembrance? As the prophetic pattern is fulfilled in each one of us, we will acknowledge God's vision and rest in this grand fact on the seventh day.

ACKNOWLEDGMENT

I would be remiss if I did not acknowledge Mary Baker Eddy and her courageous book, *Science and Health with Key to the Scriptures*, in which she reintroduced primitive Christianity to the world in the late nineteenth century. Today, her book still stands as a tower of strength to those willing to risk all for truth.

I began studying *Science and Health* when I entered college and observed it beginning to transform my view of everything. Those seeds, planted many years ago, have given me the capacity to pursue the publication of this volume, which I hope will encourage readers to pursue the book of Revelation for themselves.

George Denninger

ORGANIZATION OF THIS BOOK

Each chapter includes the Authorized King James Version of Revelation in its entirety, an explanatory introduction, and a verse-by-verse spiritual interpretation.

The Revelation

From The Holy Bible: Authorized King James Version
Format and emphasis by the author with original italics removed

Rev. 1

1 The Revelation of Jesus Christ,

which
God gave unto him,

to shew unto his servants things
which must shortly come to pass;

and he sent and signified it
by
his angel

unto his servant
John:

2 Who bare record of the word of God,
and of the testimony
of
Jesus Christ,

and of all things that he saw.

3 Blessed is he that readeth,
and they that hear the words of this prophecy,
and keep those things which are written therein:

for
the time is at hand.

4 John
to the seven churches which are in Asia:

Grace be unto you, and peace,
from him which is, and which was, and which is to
come; and
from the seven Spirits which are before his throne; And
5 **from Jesus Christ**, who is the faithful witness, and the
first begotten of the dead, and the prince of the kings of the
earth. Unto him that loved us, and washed us from our sins
in his own blood,

6 And hath made us **kings and priests** unto God and his
Father;

to him be glory and dominion for ever and ever. Amen.

7 Behold, he cometh with clouds; and every eye shall see
him, and they also which pierced him: and all kindreds of
the earth shall wail because of him.

Even so, Amen.

8 **"I am Alpha and Omega, the beginning and the**
ending," saith the Lord, "which is, and which was, and
which is to come, **the Almighty**."

9 I John, who also am your brother, and companion in
tribulation, and in the kingdom and patience of Jesus
Christ, was in the isle that is called Patmos, for the word of
God, and for the testimony of Jesus Christ.

10 I was in the Spirit on the Lord's day, and heard behind me a
great voice, as of a trumpet,
11 Saying, I am Alpha and Omega, the first and the last: and,
What thou seest, write in a book, and send it unto the seven
churches which are in Asia; unto

Ephesus, and unto
Smyrna, and unto
Pergamos, and unto
Thyatira, and unto
Sardis, and unto
Philadelphia, and unto
Laodicea.

12 And **I turned to see the voice that spake with me.** And being turned, I saw

Seven Golden Candlesticks;

13 And in the midst of the seven candlesticks

one like unto the Son of man,

clothed with a garment down to the foot, and

girt about the paps with a golden girdle.

14 His head and his hairs were white like wool, as white as snow; and

his eyes were as a flame of fire; And

15 his feet like unto fine brass, as if they burned in a furnace; and

his voice as the sound of many waters. And

16 he had in his right hand seven stars: and

out of his mouth went a sharp two-edged sword: and

his countenance was as the sun shineth in his strength.

17 And when I saw him, **I fell at his feet as dead.**

And he laid his right hand upon me, saying unto me,

18 "Fear not; I am the first and the last: I am he that liveth, and was dead; and, behold,

I am alive for evermore,"

Amen;

"and have the keys of hell and of death."

19 Write

the things which thou hast seen, and

the things which are, and

the things which shall be hereafter;

20 The mystery of the seven stars which thou sawest in my right hand, and the seven golden candlesticks.

The seven stars are the angels of the seven churches:

and the seven candlesticks which thou sawest are the seven churches.

The Revelation

John was experiencing mental metamorphosis. As he spoke in this brief introduction, the transformation developed with each passing word. His descriptions became more metaphoric as his consciousness ascended because he had no other way to describe the view. The entire revelation was passing before his vision, laying the framework for his writing of the book.

It is significant that John received this vision while still with us on earth, indicating the grand potential for all men to *be there* when the *Comforter* arrives. When we prepare ourselves as John did, we, too, will ascend to witness the apocalypse.

Title

Rev. 1

1–2 **The Revelation of Jesus Christ, which God gave unto him, to shew unto his servants things which must shortly come to pass; and he sent and signified it by his angel unto his servant John: Who bare record of the word of God, and of the testimony of Jesus Christ, and of all things that he saw.**

THE UNVEILING OF JESUS' PRESENTATION OF CHRIST
which was the gift that God gave him
to clearly show unto us the
PROPHECY AND FULFILLMENT OF MAN

This is an official document signed by its author, Jesus Christ, and presented to his servant John, who acted as a scribe and was Christ's faithful witness in recording all that he saw.

3 **Blessed is he that readeth, and they that hear the words of this prophecy, and keep those things which are written therein: for the time is at hand.**

He who reads this message and has the spiritual receptivity to hear and understand it walks forth with joy. The prophecy contained in this book is ready to be fulfilled. This is NOW!

Preface

4 **John to the seven churches which are in Asia: Grace be unto you, and peace, from him which is, and which was, and which is to come; and from the seven Spirits which are before his throne;**

From John:
To all those who have been waiting expectantly for the second coming of Christ, it is time to lift up your eyes, awaken your spiritual ears, and prepare to have the ultimate peace settle on you. The very Christ that you have witnessed before is with you now and will be with you forevermore. The whole encircling radiance of God's identity has confirmed it to me from the seat of authority.

5 **And from Jesus Christ, who is the faithful witness, and the first begotten of the dead, and the prince of the kings of the earth. Unto him that loved us, and washed us from our sins in his own blood,**

And from Jesus Christ:
Always knowing his real identity, he was the first to prove to mankind, through the loss and regaining of his own blood, that life supersedes death. His supreme sacrifice and sublime example illustrate how omnipresent Love wins the victory over sin and death in each one of us.

6 **And hath made us kings and priests unto God and his Father; to him be glory and dominion for ever and ever. Amen.**

As Jesus rose to fill the office of high priest prophesied by Moses and the office of king prophesied by David, so shall we rise to the realization of our eternal, God-given inheritance and be like him. We take off our crowns in allegiance to the only source and put on our crowns of dominion—the All-in-all of infinite good.

Amen.

7 **Behold, he cometh with clouds; and every eye shall see him, and they also which pierced him: and all kindreds of the earth shall wail because of him. Even so, Amen.**

The arrival of the Comforter appearing with clouds means that even though the potential to understand Jesus' most profound statements is fully available, that understanding is not obvious or immediately accepted at its first appearing. Regardless of whether we accept it or not, we will all be profoundly affected. Weeping and wailing at the funeral of our fondest sins, we will lose our desire for them and watch them disappear. Even our hidden hatred of truth, which would try to destroy the vision, will be forced to submit.

All Good agrees. Amen.

8 **I am Alpha and Omega, the beginning and the ending, saith the Lord, which is, and which was, and which is to come, the Almighty.**

The idea of God that appears in the sequence of *Life, Truth,* and *Love* at the beginning is understood to be *Love*, *Truth*, and *Life* at the end. We work up to the grand realization of Love, which is the impetus and finale of all. Our sense of past, present, and future is knit together in one perfect *now substance* where omnipotence reigns!

9 **I John, who also am your brother, and companion in tribulation, and in the kingdom and patience of Jesus Christ, was in the isle that is called Patmos, for the word of God, and for the testimony of Jesus Christ.**

I, John, who have no inherent advantage over you—suffering the same passions as everyone else and finding calm amidst the storm like Jesus himself demonstrated—was on the island of Patmos*, where I was placed as a living witness of Jesus Christ for the sake of the Word of God.

10–11 **I was in the Spirit on the Lord's day, and heard behind me a great voice, as of a trumpet, Saying, I am Alpha and Omega, the first and the last: and, What thou seest, write in a book, and send it unto the seven churches which are in Asia; unto Ephesus, and unto Smyrna, and unto Pergamos, and unto Thyatira, and unto Sardis, and unto Philadelphia, and unto Laodicea.**

John had set the physical senses aside and was conscious of Spirit alone, when he heard a great, penetrating voice behind him, saying, in substance, 'I am All—cause and effect.' When there are no distractions, the "still small voice" (1Kings 19:12) of truth is crystal clear and demands our full attention.

Why was the voice behind him? Even Isaiah heard the angel message from that vantage point and knew that we would too: "Thine ears shall hear a word behind thee, saying, This is the way, walk ye in it" (Isa. 30:21). We all must learn that experiencing *the Christ presence* is not an

---

* Jesus described the recognition of Christ as *the rock* upon which he would build his church. Patmos was a rock quarry. It appeared as though evil was attempting to break John's dedication, physically and figuratively, to the one rock—Christ, Truth. John was living that rock in Spirit and, therefore, was unmoved by his internment.

external event that comes to us from some distant place. John had to turn from the human way of spiritual listening, which is like a radio signal being received from a broadcasting station, to *seeing* Christ broadcast from within his very being radiating outward. Now, as a beacon, he was compelled to share the light!

The seven churches in Asia were not specific locations to send messages. Through metaphor, they illustrate advanced spiritual concepts. Since the book is written in Spirit language, we must translate the words back into the original tongue in order to understand the message. On the most basic level, we know that Asia is in the east, where the Magi first saw the star appear that would draw attention to the babe and king, Jesus. As the sun figuratively rises in the east, so the spiritual day dawns on human thought, not from Asia but from Christ. Each of the seven cities had peculiar features that help identify areas of spiritual progress and error in the evolving Christian thought. They present universal messages for mankind.

12 **And I turned to see the voice that spake with me. And being turned, I saw seven golden candlesticks;**

John changed from looking up to Spirit to looking out from Spirit; that is, he changed from being a translator of spiritual parables to living the spiritual meaning directly. As he turned, John realized the spiritual mechanism through which light shines; metaphorically, it is like seven lamp stands, seven being the symbol for completeness.

13 **And in the midst of the seven candlesticks one like unto the Son of man, clothed with a garment down to the foot, and girt about the paps with a golden girdle.**

In the center of the light bearers is the presence of an intelligent being, manifest as one like the Son of man. Jesus called himself the Son of man. This man is *like* that Son.

A robe down to the foot exemplifies the garment of a high priest and that of a king, like the seamless garment worn by Jesus. He is girded with a heart of gold—a breastplate of righteousness. This man is not identified as a specific person, but he is obviously endowed with Christly qualities. Is Jesus' angel presenting the divine prototype representing all ascended consciousness? In any event, John is about to assume the consciousness of that type of spiritualized man as his thought ascends.

14 **His head and his hairs were white like wool, as white as snow; and his eyes were as a flame of fire;**

John's ascending thought is first drawn to the focal point of intelligence, and he finds it pure white. White represents completeness, much like sunlight with its full spectrum of component colors presented as one colorless whole. This sparkling reflection of God is clean, innocent, and without shadow—not colored by human events. Eyes as fire are not cumbered about by opacity. There are no secrets here. These windows of heaven discern all good. They are not receivers of light; they radiate Christ vision out upon the universe.

15 **And his feet like unto fine brass, as if they burned in a furnace; and his voice as the sound of many waters.**

The resplendent speaker of the Word stands erect on pillars of fire, which represent foundations of Truth. Fine brass, as if burned in a furnace, is not fragmentary and brittle like the iron mixed with clay that Daniel envisioned in King Nebuchadnezzar's dream. This man has no Adam-clay component. His voice is broadcast universally. One cannot miss it or be distracted by any external voice.

16 **And he had in his right hand seven stars: and out of his mouth went a sharp two-edged sword: and his countenance was as the sun shineth in his strength.**

John's vision of man has now expanded to sun-strength radiance. The man of God's creating holds aloft the sevenfold light for all to understand while the two-edged sword of Truth delivers the Word, severing fiction from fact. A single star prophesied the Savior whose Christ light illumined the earth for all to see. Now seven stars proclaim the dawning of universal light so that all may shine like the Son of man. There will be no diluting of words any longer, no waiting for a latter day for the Comforter to arrive.

17 **And when I saw him, I fell at his feet as dead. And he laid his right hand upon me, saying unto me, Fear not; I am the first and the last:**

It was as if John was saying the following: 'When I realized the wholly spiritual nature of man, my finite sense of self died. My mistaken mortal view followed the path of Satan's fall from heaven, whereupon I witnessed error's demise. Then I was lifted up by the stellar message that touched me and took away my fear. The Christ came to where I thought I had fallen, spoke my language, and lifted me up to behold my spiritual self—whole without limits.'

"I am the first and the last." All of Revelation is condensed into this moment.

18 **I am he that liveth, and was dead; and, behold, I am alive for evermore, Amen; and have the keys of hell and of death.**

I am was always alive, even though mankind was dead to the 'I,' did not understand *I am*. Life is infinite and eternal, and this fact understood holds the key that binds hell and death. Jesus demonstrated this phenomenon and promised to send the Comforter that would open a way for all men to experience the spiritual dimension of Life, Truth, and Love.

My time is at hand (Matt. 26:18).

Directive

19 **Write the things which thou hast seen, and the things which are, and the things which shall be hereafter;**

John was told to make a permanent record of the Truth Comforter that he now understood, including the facts of existence, prophecy, and the fulfillment of man.

Key

20 **The mystery of the seven stars which thou sawest in my right hand, and the seven golden candlesticks. The seven stars are the angels of the seven churches: and the seven candlesticks which thou sawest are the seven churches.**

When presented with universal light, there are no mysteries. Stars are symbols for enlightenment, the stellar presence that God radiates out upon the universe. Candlesticks, or lamp stands, are the cumulative body from which the light shines. When these concepts are generally understood, mankind's long night of ignorance will be over.

Seven Messages Revealed

Rev. 2–3

Rev. 2

1 **Unto the angel of the church of Ephesus**
write;
These things saith
he that holdeth the seven stars in his right hand,
who walketh in the midst of the seven golden
candlesticks;

2 I know thy works, and thy labour, and thy patience, and
how thou canst not bear them which are evil: and thou hast
tried them which say they are apostles, and are not, and
hast found them liars:
3 And hast borne, and hast patience, and for my name's sake
hast laboured, and hast not fainted.
4 Nevertheless I have somewhat against thee, because

thou hast left thy FIRST LOVE.

5 Remember therefore from whence thou art fallen, and
repent, and
do the first works;
or else I will come unto thee quickly, and will remove thy
candlestick out of his place, except thou repent.
6 But this thou hast, that

thou hatest the deeds of the Nicolaitans, which I also hate.

7 He that hath an ear, let him hear what the Spirit saith unto
the churches;

To him that overcometh will I give to eat of the tree of life, which is in the midst of the paradise of God.

8 **And unto the angel of the church in Smyrna**
write;
These things saith
the first and the last,
which was dead, and is alive;

9 I know thy works, and tribulation, and poverty,
(but thou art rich)
and I know the blasphemy of them which say they are
Jews, and are not, but are the synagogue of Satan.

10 **Fear none of those things which thou shalt suffer:**

behold, the devil shall cast some of you into prison, that ye may be tried; and ye shall have tribulation ten days: be thou faithful unto death, and

I will give thee a crown of life.

11 He that hath an ear, let him hear what the Spirit saith unto the churches;
He that overcometh shall not be hurt of the second death.

---

12 **And to the angel of the church in Pergamos**
write;
These things saith
he which hath the sharp sword with two edges;

13 I know thy works, and where thou dwellest, even where Satan's seat is: and thou holdest fast my name, and hast not denied my faith, even in those days wherein Antipas was my faithful martyr, who was slain among you, where Satan dwelleth.

14 But I have a few things against thee, because
thou hast there them that hold the doctrine of Balaam,
who taught Balac to cast a stumblingblock before the
children of Israel, to eat things sacrificed unto **idols**, and to
commit **fornication**.

15 So hast thou also them that hold the **doctrine of the**
Nicolaitans, which thing I hate.

16 **Repent**; or else
I will come unto thee quickly, and
will fight against them with the sword of my mouth.

17 He that hath an ear, let him hear what the Spirit saith unto the churches;

To him that overcometh will I give to eat of the hidden manna, and will give him a white stone, and in the stone a new name written, which no man knoweth saving he that receiveth it.

---

18 **And unto the angel of the church in Thyatira**
write;
These things saith the Son of God, who hath
his eyes like unto a flame of fire, and
his feet are like fine brass;

19 I know thy ***works***, and **charity**, and **service**, and **faith**, and
thy **patience**, and thy ***works;*** and the last to be more than
the first.
20 Notwithstanding I have a few things against thee, because
thou sufferest that woman Jezebel, which calleth herself
a prophetess, to teach and to seduce my servants to
commit fornication, and to eat things sacrificed unto
idols.

21 And I gave her space to repent of her fornication; and she
repented not.
22 Behold, **I will cast her into a bed**, and them that commit
adultery with her into great tribulation, except they repent
of their deeds. And
23 **I will kill her children with death**; and
all the churches shall know that
I am he which searcheth the reins and hearts:
and I will give unto every one of you according to your
works.
24 But unto you I say, and unto the rest in Thyatira, as many
as have not this doctrine, and which have not known the
depths of Satan, as they speak; I will put upon you none
other burden.
25 But that which ye have already

hold fast till I come.

26–27 **And he that overcometh, and keepeth my works unto
the end, to him will I give power over the nations: And
he shall rule them with a rod of iron; as the vessels of a
potter shall they be broken to shivers: even as I received
of my Father.**

28 **And I will give him the morning star.**
29 He that hath an ear, let him hear what the Spirit saith unto
the churches.

Rev. 3

1 **And unto the angel of the church in Sardis**
write;
These things saith
**he that hath the seven Spirits of God, and
the seven stars;**

I know thy works, that
thou hast a name that thou livest, and art dead.

2 Be ***watchful***, and **strengthen** the things which remain, that
are ready to die: for
I have not found thy works perfect before God.

3 **Remember** therefore how thou hast received and heard,
and **hold fast**, and **repent**.
If therefore thou shalt not ***watch***, I will come on thee as a
thief, and thou shalt not know what hour I will come upon
thee.
4 Thou hast a few names even in Sardis which have not
defiled their garments; and they shall walk with me in
white: for they are worthy.

5 **He that overcometh, the same shall be clothed in white
raiment; and
I will not blot out his name out of the book of life, but
I will confess his name before my Father, and before his
angels.**

6 He that hath an ear, let him hear what the Spirit saith unto
the churches.

---

7 **And to the angel of the church in Philadelphia**
write;
These things saith
he that is holy,
he that is true,
he that hath the key of David,
**he that openeth, and no man shutteth; and
shutteth, and no man openeth;**

8 I know thy works: behold, I have set before thee an **open
door**, and no man can shut it: for
**thou hast a little strength, and hast kept my word,
and hast not denied my name.**

9 Behold, I will make them of the synagogue of Satan, which
say they are Jews, and are not, but do lie; behold, I will

make them to come and worship before thy feet, and to
know that **I have loved thee.**

10 Because thou hast kept the word of my patience, I also will
keep thee from the hour of temptation, which shall come
upon all the world, to try them that dwell upon the earth.
11 Behold, I come quickly: hold that fast which thou hast, that
no man take thy crown.

12 Him that overcometh will I

make a pillar in the temple of my God, and he shall go no more out: and

I will write upon him the name of my God, and the name of the city of my God, which is new Jerusalem, which cometh down out of heaven from my God: and

I will write upon him my new name.

13 He that hath an ear, let him hear what the Spirit saith unto the churches.

---

14 **And unto the angel of the church of the Laodiceans** write;
These things saith

the Amen,
the faithful and true witness,
the beginning of the creation of God;

15 I know thy works,

that thou art neither cold nor hot:

I would thou wert cold or hot.

16 So then because thou art lukewarm, and neither cold nor hot, **I will spue thee out of my mouth.**

17 **Because thou sayest, I am rich,**
and increased with goods, and
have need of nothing;
and knowest not that thou art
wretched, and miserable, and
poor, and blind, and naked:

18 I counsel thee to **buy of me**
gold tried in the fire, that thou mayest be rich; and

white raiment, that thou mayest be clothed, and that the shame of thy nakedness do not appear; and anoint thine eyes with eyesalve, that thou mayest see.

19 **As many as I love, I rebuke and chasten:**

be **zealous** therefore, and **repent**.

20 Behold, I stand at the door, and knock: if any man hear my voice, and open the door, I will come in to him, and will sup with him, and he with me.

21 **To him that overcometh will I grant to sit with me in my throne, even as I also overcame, and am set down with my Father in his throne.**

22 He that hath an ear, let him hear what the Spirit saith unto the churches.

Seven Messages Revealed

The Christ, Truth, that presents itself as a particular message for each church is the same Elohim (God) that is recorded in the first chapter of Genesis. The particular name for God that is required in each case offers the solution for that church. Comparing the particular name to the activities therein makes the error, the tools for reform, the solution, and the prize glaringly apparent. Like the facets of a diamond, each message is complete unto itself, and its substance is identical to the whole.

The Essence of the Messages to the Seven Churches

(1st) Ephesus
If you suppose that you can lose your *light, Life*,

(2nd) Smyrna
then you believe in another god besides Me.

(3rd) Pergamos
You will experience the finite first as matter

(4th) Thyatira
and then as a mortal mind.

To find your way back home, what you supposed must be unlearned.

(5th) Sardis
To do this, you must *watch* with conviction.

(6th) Philadelphia
The unction of *Love* is the way, and you can feel it enough to follow.

(7th) Laodicea
When you get near the boundaries of the finite, the dreadful mistake will seem insurmountable, and that mistake will increasingly torment you until infinite Love turns you—the dream loses its illusion and disappears.

We spend our mortal lives in these steps until there is no *mortal*.

Message 1 — to those who think like Ephesus

Rev. 2

1 **Unto the angel of the church of Ephesus write; These things saith he that holdeth the seven stars in his right hand, who walketh in the midst of the seven golden candlesticks;**

My angel wrote this from the beginning: "Let there be light: and there was light" (Gen. 1:3). 'I' manifest the infinite power of that light, radiating it freely throughout the allness of my being. Realize that you emanate that light as 'I' do. The structure of Truth and Love that is you abides with Me and is like Me, manifesting the presence of that light. Make a permanent record of it.

2–3 **I know thy works, and thy labour, and thy patience, and how thou canst not bear them which are evil: and thou hast tried them which say they are apostles, and are not, and hast found them liars: And hast borne, and hast patience, and for my name's sake hast laboured, and hast not fainted.**

Humanly, I can see your earnest attempts at discipleship, your patient waiting, your hatred of hypocrisy, and your courage in attempting to expunge that error.

4 **Nevertheless I have somewhat against thee, because thou hast left thy FIRST LOVE.**

I applaud you for your vigor, but I also know where you are falling short. You have forgotten the cause that underlies your purpose—light, enlightenment.

5 **Remember therefore from whence thou art fallen, and repent, and do the first works; or else I will come unto thee quickly, and will remove thy candlestick out of his place, except thou repent.**

If you do not remember the spiritual way, you will experience the problem until the solution appears. Losing your light, you experience darkness. Ruminating and grumbling with fits and starts, you will struggle to regain what was lost until you discover that 'I' am right here, ready to re-establish and correct your perceptions.

6 **But this thou hast, that thou hatest the deeds of the Nicolaitans, which I also hate.**

I am glad you understand that spiritual speech and immoral practice do not mix. Degenerate behavior is deplorable.

7 **He that hath an ear, let him hear what the Spirit saith unto the churches; To him that overcometh will I give to eat of the tree of life, which is in the midst of the paradise of God.**

Infinite God supplies infinite light, not finite *things*, not better human situations or relationships. Never, at any moment, seek the things. Never claim the things as personal possessions. The light of Life is instantaneous. There is no interval between "*He spake,* and *it was done*" (Ps. 33:9). 'I' gave you that light. Listen with that light!

When you recognize how truth works and bear that light, your immediate prize is the Tree of Life, which includes all—the center and circumference of being.

Message 2 — to those who think like Smyrna

8–9 **And unto the angel of the church in Smyrna write; These things saith the first and the last, which was dead, and is alive; I know thy works, and tribulation, and poverty, (but thou art rich) and I know the blasphemy of them which say they are Jews, and are not, but are the synagogue of Satan.**

Write this in your mind: *I am* from before until hereafter. Even though you were dead to Me, 'I,' Christ, am here. With your limited sense of life, you are having partial victories, but you also experience the turmoil and poverty of that limited life. From the point of perfection, some of your attempts at worship are nothing more than a charade.

10 **Fear none of those things which thou shalt suffer: behold, the devil shall cast some of you into prison, that ye may be tried; and ye shall have tribulation ten days: be thou faithful unto death, and I will give thee a crown of life.**

Is there any reality or power other than God? To those who think so, 'I' wrote The Ten Commandments, for "thou shalt have no other gods before me" (Exod. 20:3). Each Commandment will judge you and trouble you and guide you until you have mastered its true meaning.

Your humility and dedication to Christ have brought you this far. Tribulation comes because you are unsure about what you say. If God did not say it, why should anyone believe you? Your disappointment, which you yourself have occasioned, makes you feel poor and anxious. Ensconced in a material universe, you feel stuck in a sensual body. As long as there is some *thing* to destroy, it will be attacked, and your best efforts will result in persecution. Know this: you will stop being persecuted when the persecution ceases

Change your standpoint: leave the Adam curse behind. Christ divides asunder truth from error, persistently knocking on your conscience while providing useful, right activity.

17 **He that hath an ear, let him hear what the Spirit saith unto the churches; To him that overcometh will I give to eat of the hidden manna, and will give him a white stone, and in the stone a new name written, which no man knoweth saving he that receiveth it.**

Morally perceptive humanity senses Life outside of limitation and hungrily probes for a new definition without limits. Remember Jacob who wrestled with the angel, persevered, and was given his new name, Israel? So must you give up your passive acceptance of a material sense of things, eat the hidden manna (God substance), and listen with ears that surpass material function as Soul identifies itself. Then you will know the truth, but you will not be able to share it because there is no human method of transmitting spiritual identity.

Message 4 — to those who think like Thyatira

18 **And unto the angel of the church in Thyatira write; These things saith the Son of God, who hath his eyes like unto a flame of fire, and his feet are like fine brass;**

Write this message to those who tolerate an evil mind and thereby allow themselves to be so influenced: Christ is the all-seeing Mind, gleaming within and without, standing in perfect refinement and searching the reins and hearts.

19 **I know thy works, and charity, and service, and faith, and thy patience, and thy works; and the last to be more than the first.**

The milk of the Word leads to sharing, and sharing leads to service, and service leads to faith, and faith grows into patient practice. Practice, as a living faith, is a greater work than the object of your first lessons.

20 **Notwithstanding I have a few things against thee, because thou sufferest that woman Jezebel, which calleth herself a prophetess, to teach and to seduce my servants to commit fornication, and to eat things sacrificed unto idols.**

The serpent's lure, hiding behind the veil of a clean facade, has less-than-pure motives. Beneath the footprint of material form lurks the mentality of a serpent. Indulging in a clever intellect is impressive to your fellow mortals, but not to the all-seeing Mind.

21–22 **And I gave her space to repent of her fornication; and she repented not. Behold, I will cast her into a bed, and them that commit adultery with her into great tribulation, except they repent of their deeds.**

If you know how hypocrisy is boastful and yet still continue to tolerate and practice it, then you will suffer and fall because you cannot hear my voice. You have not reached the heights of heaven because you have not plumbed the depths of hell and cleaned it out. Belief in a mind separate from God must be overthrown.

> For the punishment of the iniquity of the daughter of my people is greater than the punishment of the sin of Sodom, that was overthrown as in a moment, and no hands stayed on her (Lam. 4:6).

23 **And I will kill her children with death; and all the churches shall know that I am he which searcheth the reins and hearts: and I will give unto every one of you according to your works.**

Attempting to motivate yourself or others through a sense of personal holiness makes you a hypocrite. Everything you teach that way is lost, and so are you.

24 **But unto you I say, and unto the rest in Thyatira, as many as have not this doctrine, and which have not known the depths of Satan, as they speak; I will put upon you none other burden.**

This one lesson is, indeed, sufficient for you: understand your way out of the evil suggestions inherent in mortal mind.

25 **But that which ye have already hold fast till I come.**

If you already know something of truth, cling to it with all your might, and that good seed will grow into divine freedom.

26–27 **And he that overcometh, and keepeth my works unto the end, to him will I give power over the nations: And he shall rule them with a rod of iron; as the vessels of a potter shall they be broken to shivers: even as I received of my Father.**

To those of you who were ignorant of your mental mistakes but have now become aware and repentant, hold fast to what you have learned. You must strive to master these insidious hidden evils in yourselves, until everyone in the world breaks the fetters of believing in a mind apart from God. Your old beliefs will eventually be seen as fragmentary notions without entity, for God alone governs man.

28 **And I will give him the morning star.**

My light will dawn upon you and all.

29 **He that hath an ear, let him hear what the Spirit saith unto the churches.**

Real identity is wholly spiritual. Listen that way.

Message 5 — to those who think like Sardis

Rev. 3

1 **And unto the angel of the church in Sardis write; These things saith he that hath the seven Spirits of God, and the seven stars; I know thy works, that thou hast a name that thou livest, and art dead.**

I can see your perfection and know you by name, but you are lulled to sleep by the senses and are dead to these facts. From where you are now, you will not be able to proceed without prophecy, so I will provide it. First, I present the full spectrum of God (all seven Spirits radiating *Us*) so that you will know that you and 'I' are not separate. Second, I present all seven messages to all seven churches before you ask and before you copy them down. The seven star-messengers are already shining my glory.

2 **Be watchful, and strengthen the things which remain, that are ready to die: for I have not found thy works perfect before God.**

You must foresee the end of evil and work it out with what you know to be true. Earnestly watch for the obstacles of matter to disappear, including the limitations of the physical senses.

3 **Remember therefore how thou hast received and heard, and hold fast, and repent. If therefore thou shalt not watch, I will come on thee as a thief, and thou shalt not know what hour I will come upon thee.**

Remember how prophecy always precedes fulfillment on earth? If you are not keeping constant watch, when fulfillment comes you will miss it, and you may even misinterpret the event and fight against spiritual progress. My glory feels like hell to the unprepared and uninitiated.

The door will open. Will you be ready?

4 **Thou hast a few names even in Sardis which have not defiled their garments; and they shall walk with me in white: for they are worthy.**

Innocence already knows its inheritance.

5 **He that overcometh, the same shall be clothed in white raiment; and I will not blot out his name out of the book of life, but I will confess his name before my Father, and before his angels.**

Those who have erred but turned away from it, who have watched and overcome those difficulties, are clean every whit, just as the innocent are. Watch and hold fast, and I foresee and foresay your names signified in the book of Life, which is so essential to leaving the old landmarks and ascending beyond the illusion and memory of death and hell.

6 **He that hath an ear, let him hear what the Spirit saith unto the churches.**

Listen with a watchful ear, and you will always know before it comes to pass. In heaven, the work is already done.

Message 6 — to those who think like Philadelphia

7 **And to the angel of the church in Philadelphia write; These things saith he that is holy, he that is true, he that hath the key of David, he that openeth, and no man shutteth; and shutteth, and no man openeth;**

Truth and Love, the essence of holiness, is the key that David prophesied would forever open the door to Christ likeness. Even though brainpower can neither discover nor understand the key, use what intelligence you have to record this message so that when man learns what Love is this prophecy will be realized.

8 **I know thy works: behold, I have set before thee an open door, and no man can shut it: for thou hast a little strength, and hast kept my word, and hast not denied my name.**

Sweet Philadelphia, you know the essence of Me.
I presented the key to you, and with it you have unlocked my treasure. Indeed, Love is the simplest and most profound of Me and is the true way to all that is.

> Blessed are the pure in heart: for they shall see God (Matt. 5:8).

9 **Behold, I will make them of the synagogue of Satan, which say they are Jews, and are not, but do lie; behold, I will make them to come and worship before thy feet, and to know that I have loved thee.**

What you know of Love, in your simple way, has opened the door and set the sublime example on earth. Love is so powerful that even those with wicked pretence will eventually be cleansed, come to the same conclusion that you have, and thank you.

10 **Because thou hast kept the word of my patience, I also will keep thee from the hour of temptation, which shall come upon all the world, to try them that dwell upon the earth.**

Because you have learned how to abide by grace in divine Love, when temptation and distress of nations come, you will be so conscious of Me that you will not even notice.

11 **Behold, I come quickly: hold that fast which thou hast, that no man take thy crown.**

Cling to Love, and you will lose your earthly weights without a struggle. No one will be able to make you forget who you really are because you are the crown of my glory. Universal Love never wavers.

12 **Him that overcometh will I make a pillar in the temple of my God, and he shall go no more out: and I will write upon him the name of my God, and the name of the city of my God, which is new Jerusalem, which cometh down out of heaven from my God: and I will write upon him my new name.**

Those who love their way past their fears will find that as they ascend, inspired fleeting moments increase in frequency until spiritual living is realized permanently.

You will recognize your true identity in this way:

- Standing in the firmament of heaven, you will discover your identity to be God consciousness.
- New Jerusalem will be found to be here and everywhere, encompassing the all of your being.
- Divine Love will explain itself—“Behold, I make all things new” (Rev. 21:5).

13 **He that hath an ear, let him hear what the Spirit saith unto the churches.**

Keep your ears open to the key—Love.

Message 7 — to those who think like Laodicea

14 **And unto the angel of the church of the Laodiceans write; These things saith the Amen, the faithful and true witness, the beginning of the creation of God;**

From the *Amen* ascension to before the world was, ‘I’ am ever present. The ‘I’ of Life, Truth, and Love is always right in front of your face and is the reality of your being. Even though you are superficially aware of this fact, intellectual knowledge of my presence is not enough. You need to record my presence with practical proofs.

15–18 **I know thy works, that thou art neither cold nor hot: I would thou wert cold or hot. So then because thou art lukewarm, and neither cold nor hot, I will spue thee out of my mouth. Because thou sayest, I am rich, and increased with goods, and have need of nothing; and knowest not that thou art wretched, and miserable, and poor, and blind, and naked: I counsel thee to buy of me gold tried in the fire, that thou mayest be rich; and white raiment, that thou mayest be clothed, and that the shame of thy nakedness do not appear; and anoint thine eyes with eyesalve, that thou mayest see.**

You sit there half-asleep, satisfied with an intellectual understanding of God that you ignore and a sense of personal accomplishment and pleasure that you embrace, all the while disregarding your neighbors' needs. If you do not love them, you certainly do not know *Me*! You have been apathetic, lethargic, idle, dull, weak, drunk, careless, ungrateful, indecisive, and wishy-washy, fooled by the serpent into believing you have a choice of good or evil and loving it. You are self-indulgent, self-satisfied, lacking in moral conviction, and foolishly seeking security in matter. 'I' have dominion over your blindness and nakedness, and you know it, yet you fail because you are lackadaisically neutral. What a loss!

In the beginning, 'I' coddled you with milk, healing you and telling you parables because you were too immature to swallow the truth. Now it is time to eat the meat. Remember when 'I' said, "Word was made flesh"? (John 1:14). 'I' have tried to give you the meat before, and I repeated it in my Philadelphia message. Why are you not chewing on it? You have not even tried to digest what 'I' said. Did you not hear Me when 'I' said that you are my sons and daughters?

My Word is Life, and that life is sinless. My presence is your bounty. Clothe yourself with My innocence, and you will neither be ashamed nor guilty. Your home, which is all around you right now, is holy. See it with the eyes 'I' gave you.

19 **As many as I love, I rebuke and chasten: be zealous therefore, and repent.**

I would not talk to you like this if I did not love you and expect you to recover. Strive to understand divine Love until love owns you.

20 **Behold, I stand at the door, and knock: if any man hear my voice, and open the door, I will come in to him, and will sup with him, and he with me.**

'I' am right here knocking at the door of your conscience. If you are hungering for the truth and can stop your foolishness and be still, you will know my presence: 'I' in you and you in Me.

21 **To him that overcometh will I grant to sit with me in my throne, even as I also overcame, and am set down with my Father in his throne.**

At the end of this so-called pathway to righteousness is total dominion. I have set the example and opened the way for you to follow. You are all kings and priests unto God, united as One, Spirit, Life, Truth, Love. Sitting with Me on the throne is your ultimate inheritance.

22 **He that hath an ear, let him hear what the Spirit saith unto the churches.**

These messages are delivered and written in Spirit language, and you have the ability to receive them. Are you listening with spiritual ears?

Vision 1

THE THRONE

Rev. 4

1 After this I looked, and, behold, **a door was opened in heaven**: and the first voice which I heard was as it were of a trumpet talking with me; which said,

"**Come up hither**,
and I will shew thee things which must be hereafter."

2 And immediately I was in the spirit:

and, behold, a throne was set in heaven, and

ONE sat on THE THRONE.

3 And he that sat was to look upon like a jasper and a sardine stone:

and there was a **rainbow** round about the throne, in sight like unto an emerald.

4 And round about the throne were **four and twenty seats**: and upon the seats I saw **four and twenty elders** sitting, clothed in **white raiment**; and they had on their heads **crowns of gold**.

5 And out of the throne proceeded lightnings and thunderings and voices:

and there were **seven lamps of fire** burning before the throne, which are the **seven Spirits of God**.

6 And before the throne there was a **sea of glass** like unto crystal:

and in the midst of the throne, and round about the throne, were **four beasts full of eyes before and behind**.

7 And the first beast was **like a lion**, and
the second beast **like a calf**, and
the third beast had **a face as a man**, and
the fourth beast was **like a flying eagle**.

8 And the four beasts had each of them **six wings** about him;
and they were **full of eyes within**: and they rest not day and
night, saying,

"Holy, holy, holy, Lord God Almighty, which was, and is, and is to come."

9 And when those beasts give glory and honour and thanks to
him that sat on the throne, who liveth for ever and ever,

10 The four and twenty elders
fall down before him that sat on the throne, and
worship him that liveth for ever and ever, and
cast their crowns before the throne, saying,

11 Thou art worthy, O Lord, to receive glory and honour and
power: for thou hast created all things, and for thy pleasure
they are and were created.

The Throne—God

Rev. 4

We cannot comprehend a mathematical principle without illustrating it with numerals and mathematical processes, and we do not understand it until we put it into practice. As it is with mathematics, so it is with metaphysics.

It is obvious that the spiritual infinite cannot be described in finite forms; however, the principle that underlies all form and action may be hinted at by symbolically illustrating the manifestation and creative processes of that principle. This chapter is a symbol of God's presence, a compound illustration of God as One in which Spirit defines itself. We must drop physical musings and look at spiritually animated thought. Human visualization under physical law prevents us from accepting the idea that things can be in two different places at the same time; nevertheless, this is normal in heaven, where there is "time no longer" (Rev. 10:6). Also, bear in mind that because the infinite cannot be delineated, there is no sense of scale or measurement.

1... **After this I looked, and, behold, a door was opened in heaven: and the first voice which I heard was as it were of a trumpet talking with me;**

John is a wise virgin, for Love has opened the door of his waiting thought. Furthermore, it is apparent that he is not a spiritual beginner. In the early stages of spiritual growth, in the quiet of conscience, we hear the "still small voice" of Spirit telling us what *not* to do. A consciousness refined and enhanced by practice hears a loud and compelling message, usually commanding something positive *to* do. For John, the initial message piercing through space is as a trumpet commanding him to come up and see!

…1 **which said, Come up hither, and I will shew thee things which must be hereafter.**
2… **And immediately I was in the spirit:**

The call to "come up hither" is not a call to move to another place or another dimension; it is a call to leave the faulty knowledge of this world behind—to come out and be separate. This is the only way to begin to grasp the knowledge of God.

> Wherefore come out from among them, and be ye separate, saith the Lord, and touch not the unclean thing; and I will receive you, And will be a Father unto you, and ye shall be my sons and daughters, saith the Lord Almighty (2 Cor. 6:17–18).

John complied: he came out and was received. It is also evident that he assumed the nature of divine manifestation. As stated in the passage, "Let there be light: and there was light," where cause and effect are instant and combined, John hears the call to come up hither and immediately is out of matter consciousness and is in spiritual form. He is not doing this of himself but is recognizing his transformed nature spiritually, no longer limited by finiteness.

Based on his description, John is an observer with a grand field of view, witnessing this momentous compound presence. Ultimately, it is imperative to know where he is located in the vision, but first we need to understand the symbols of the throne and its surroundings. Remember, Jesus Christ is presenting this Revelation. Without Christ, there is no revealing of God.

…2 **and, behold, a throne was set in heaven, and one sat on the throne.**

John sees one central throne from which everything else is encircling and radiating, and one sitting on the throne, figuratively commanding the scene with supreme authority.

There is none other. One cause can have but one presentation of itself, and this one presentation is required. Mind must think, Life must live, Love must love, for cause must have effect in order to be cause. The figure on the throne is the primal effect of God—His one image.

3... **And he that sat was to look upon like a jasper and a sardine stone:**

Sardine stone is the first stone in the high priest's breastplate. Since jasper is a multicolored rock, it can represent all colors. Jesus referred to Peter's recognition of the Christ as the stone (*petros)* upon which he would build his church (*temple)*. The temple he rebuilt in three days was his body. Therefore, this one sitting on the throne is identical to or at one with the Christ man—the two primal identifiers being *one* and *all* (first stone and all colors), or *All-in-all*. Paul echoed this thought.

> That the God of our Lord Jesus Christ, the Father of glory, may give unto you the spirit of wisdom and revelation in the knowledge of him: . . . And hath put all things under his feet, and gave him to be the head over all things to the church, Which is his body, the fulness of him that filleth all in all (Eph. 1:17, 22–23).

...3 **and there was a rainbow round about the throne, in sight like unto an emerald.**

A full circle rainbow can only be seen where there is no obstacle to block it. When standing on the earth, we only see the top half. Peering out the window of an airplane and looking toward earth, we sometimes see this full circle bow, and it always encircles us. The rainbow in John's vision is also round about *the observer,* which is an important clue to John's location.

In ancient Hebrew, the word *emerald* means lightning and shining. Emeralds are usually green in color, but the most precious ones are transparent. This rainbow charged with light also embraced Noah in his day, a clear signal of God's abiding love for his children.

As we recognize and assume our royal inheritance as sons and daughters of God, we, too, will see this shining bow round about us.

4 **And round about the throne were four and twenty seats: and upon the seats I saw four and twenty elders sitting, clothed in white raiment; and they had on their heads crowns of gold.**

The twenty-four elders present an exquisite and inclusive idea of their dual nature as kings and priests unto God. In Scripture, twelve means complete—all, everything, everyone, etcetera—and it always refers to something good. There are several possible explanations for twice twelve, yet if we consider that the elders have a dual nature, perhaps we are seeing twelve and its reflection.

Their first nature is illustrated here by elders sitting on seats surrounding the throne, as a king's court. Elders are known for their maturity, dignity, experience, and honor. They are not formal priests elected to office but are known by their works. Jesus typified the work of an elder, claiming no authority other than God. As the lion of the tribe of Judah from which the kings came, he fulfilled David's prophecy that *my Lord* would come from the same God-ordained root and be exalted to the throne by the same divine ordination. In like manner, the twelve apostles sat down with him as elders-in-training. The God-ordained thoughts that the apostles received were pure gold written in their foreheads and worn as crowns.

Ideas that are ready to act on every impulse of God's directing are the type that sit on the seats, wear the crowns of gold on their heads, and dress in white raiment (signifying victory, purity, and a wholly spiritual presence). These elders are royal responders.

5... **And out of the throne proceeded lightnings and thunderings and voices:**

And the Word was with God, and the Word was God (John 1:1).

Spiritual sense as Word proceeds from the center and is unmistakably vibrant, illustrating the fundamental nature of creation with ever-expanding and clearer tones. At Jesus' crucifixion, some heard thunder while the more enlightened said an angel spoke to him. Enthroned elders always hear the message clearly and repeat it, for there is no other voice.

...5 **and there were seven lamps of fire burning before the throne, which are the seven Spirits of God.**

Mathematically, seven is a prime number, indivisible by any other number except itself and the number one. As mentioned earlier, it stands for *all, whole,* and *complete*. In Genesis, creation was finished in seven days. Jesus cast out seven devils from Mary, meaning he cast out all devils.

The identity of God (spiritual cause) is symbolized here as seven lamps of fire. These seven Spirits are divine titles. Seven synonymous terms for God named in Scripture are Spirit, Life, Truth, Love, Soul, Mind, and—the one most implied though not translated directly—Principle. In Latin, *Alpha* is *principio,* from which our word *principle* is derived. In Genesis 1:1, the word rendered *beginning* in the King James Bible is also *principio.* Genesis 1 could read, 'In *Principle* God created the heaven and the earth.'

6... **And before the throne there was a sea of glass like unto crystal:**

The sea of glass is still and flat with infinite range, and it is absolutely transparent like crystal. It is flat because there is nothing to disturb the waters: no winds, no tempest-tossed waves, and no tidal pull from gravitational attraction. When Christ stilled the tempest, "there was a great calm" (Matt. 8:26).

> Every valley shall be exalted, and every mountain and hill shall be made low: and the crooked shall be made straight, and the rough places plain (Isa. 40:4).

There are no secrets here, no mountainous obstacles or fears, no depressing valleys or woes. Everything is seen in infinite resolution, and all is good. The sea of glass is the arena where "God saw every thing that he had made, and, behold, it was very good" (Gen. 1:31). This sea is *thought* seen as the universe of Mind: Mind's one song.

…6 **and in the midst of the throne, and round about the**
throne, were four beasts full of eyes before and behind.
7–8 **And the first beast was like a lion, and the second beast**
like a calf, and the third beast had a face as a man, and
the fourth beast was like a flying eagle. And the four
beasts had each of them six wings about him; and they
were full of eyes within: and they rest not day and
night, saying, Holy, holy, holy, Lord God Almighty,
which was, and is, and is to come.

The four beasts in the midst and round about the throne are more correctly translated as four living beings; of course, they have no animal qualities because there is no dimensional form as Spirit. They appear at the same moment to be in the center and at the circumference. God is *everywhere,* and so are these characteristics. They are like a lion, a calf, a face as a man, and a flying eagle. These so-called beings are ancient biblical symbols, described similarly in Ezekiel and Daniel, and they represent the following qualities: the magnificent vitality of the lion stands for strength and power; the calf, or young ox, is worshipped as a god for manifesting knowledge, or science; the man is the one who is aware of all, or has the presence of all; and the eagle is the one lifted up who is ever active. Therefore, these living beings stand for *omnipotence, omniscience, omnipresence,* and *omni-action*—all characteristics of God's nature. They are full of eyes before, behind, and within. Nothing escapes their gaze because they are *all-seeing.*

The four beasts each have six wings. Resist the temptation to visualize feathers and strange attachments, and think of Cartesian coordinates. From any point of reference, they can move north, south, east, west, up, or down—they are *omnidirectional.* These are the living beings' six-winged capabilities. And what of their purpose? Three times, the universal qualities of God ring out, "Holy, holy, holy," thwarting evil's three attempts to *be like Him,* and in every case—past, present, and future—NOW IS!

9–11 **And when those beasts give glory and honour and thanks to him that sat on the throne, who liveth for ever and ever, The four and twenty elders fall down before him that sat on the throne, and worship him that liveth for ever and ever, and cast their crowns before the throne, saying, Thou art worthy, O Lord, to receive glory and honour and power: for thou hast created all things, and for thy pleasure they are and were created.**

The reflex images of the elders are supremely adept at worshipping. Moses identified and lived the office of high priest, and he wisely prophesied that the Messiah would be like unto him. Jesus answered the call, arriving at the altar as "the lamb slain from the foundation of the world" (Rev. 13:8). Moses also foresaw that the twelve tribes of Israel would enter the Promised Land with the commandments written in their hearts, a requirement of high priests. Therefore, the twenty-four elders have characteristics of both king and priest. This dual purpose is even more evident when we realize that because the four living beings never stop praising, the elders never stop worshipping. They are falling off their seats, taking off their crowns, and listening; and simultaneously, sitting on their seats, wearing crowns, and singing. Jesus' comment, "I can of mine own self do nothing," was made with his crown off, and "as I hear, I judge" was made with his crown on (John 5:30).

With perfect humility, waiting on God and being none other, we *hear* the Word, are one with the Word, and *speak* the Word: "For by grace are ye saved through faith; and that not of yourselves: it is the gift of God" (Eph. 2:8). Identity is established by this dual state, thinking in unison as the Mind of God.

Where is John as the observer and faithful witness to this grand view of God?

> To him that overcometh will I grant to sit with me in my throne, even as I also overcame, and am set down with my Father in his throne (Rev. 3:21).

To be as one on the throne is the final reward stated in the last message to the seventh church. Jesus called himself the *Son of man,* and his prophetic call to all mankind is to be like him, *where he is*. John's mental state is "like unto the Son of man" (Rev. 1:13, 14:14). It is important to understand that the entire compound symbol being presented is John's mental state. John is living the *now* moment from one to all. As described later in Revelation, he sees multitudes standing on the sea of glass, and they are all incredibly beautiful and perfect, just as he is. This is his singular view of the universe.

Translating that presence of God for each one of us, every individual manifestation of God is the one sitting on the throne looking out upon the universe and witnessing everyone else on the sea of glass. This is a perfect projection of ascended man, and the infinite cause underlying it is one God.

Vision 1

THE SEALED BOOK AND THE LAMB

Rev. 5

1 And I saw in the right hand of him that sat on the throne
A BOOK
written within and on the backside,
SEALED WITH SEVEN SEALS.

2 And I saw a strong angel proclaiming with a loud voice,

"Who is worthy to open the book,
and to loose the seals thereof?"

3 And no man in heaven, nor in earth, neither under the earth,
was able to open the book, neither to look thereon.

4 And I wept much, because no man was found worthy to
open and to read the book, neither to look thereon.

5 And one of the elders saith unto me,
"Weep not: behold,
the Lion of the tribe of Juda,
the Root of David, hath prevailed
to open the book, and
to loose the seven seals thereof."

6 And I beheld, and, lo, in the midst of the throne and of the
four beasts, and in the midst of the elders, stood
a Lamb as it had been slain,
having **seven horns** and **seven eyes**, which are the seven
Spirits of God sent forth into all the earth.

7 And he came and took the book out of the right hand of
him that sat upon the throne.
8 And when he had taken the book, the four beasts and four
and twenty elders fell down before the Lamb, having every
one of them harps, and golden vials full of odours, which
are the prayers of saints.

9 **And they sung a new song**, saying,
"Thou art worthy to take the book, and to open the seals thereof:
for thou wast slain, and hast redeemed us to God by thy blood out of every kindred, and tongue, and people, and nation;
10 *And hast made us unto our God kings and priests:*
and we shall reign on the earth."

11 And I beheld, and I heard the voice of many angels round
about the throne and the beasts and the elders: and the
number of them was ten thousand times ten thousand, and
thousands of thousands;
12 Saying with a loud voice,
"Worthy is the Lamb that was slain to receive power, and
riches, and wisdom, and strength, and honour, and glory,
and blessing."

13 And every creature which is in heaven, and on the earth,
and under the earth, and such as are in the sea, and all that
are in them,
heard **I** saying,
"Blessing, and honour, and glory, and power, be unto him
that sitteth upon the throne, and unto the Lamb for ever and
ever."

14 And the four beasts said,
"Amen."

And the four and twenty elders fell down and worshipped
him that liveth for ever and ever.

Vision 1

The Sealed Book and the Lamb—Christ

Rev. 5

Defining *Christ* appears to be a difficult assignment, for it is impossible to deduce spiritual consciousness from the physical senses. Even the human mind is incapable of understanding how it is possible for man to know God. Psychology invents hypotheses, and pathological religion builds idols and hopes for the best, but these methods end where they began—with questions. The answers are sealed (unreadable) because mankind starts from the wrong vantage point—his. In chapter 4, we read that in heaven everything proceeds from or is round about the throne; in other words, everything proceeds from Mind (God) and is surrounded by Mind's qualities and universe. Therefore, the only way to know the mechanism of Christ is to be there, sitting on the throne, where we can witness Mind's operation for ourselves. Then when we are ready, Christ presents the knowledge of God's operation to us in a form that we can understand.

In John's day, wax seals were used on books and scrolls to assure privacy and to identify the person who did the sealing. A king would secure his important, private communications with his personal stamp. No one was allowed to open a sealed document except the person identified. In this metaphor, the book is sealed by God and sent to Christ. The message appears from the throne and is received by the one sitting on the throne. That is why we must watch from that same perspective in order to understand Christ.

1 **And I saw in the right hand of him that sat on the throne a book written within and on the backside, sealed with seven seals.**

John saw how mightily Mind protects its own wisdom. Without the proper vantage point offered by Christ, both inner and outer vision is permanently blocked. Without Christ, we would have no conscience (no cognition of good) and prophecy would serve no purpose because no one would watch for its fulfillment. Between conscience and physical sense, "there is a great gulf fixed" (Luke 16:26). Christ-inspired writing must be unsealed before it can become inspired reading!

2 **And I saw a strong angel proclaiming with a loud voice, Who is worthy to open the book, and to loose the seals thereof?**

This is a God question that does not require an answer from us. Since the Word is the only voice in the universe of Mind, the presence of God asks and answers all questions. Omnipotence, omniscience, omnipresence, and omni-action have eyes before, behind, and within.

3 **And no man in heaven, nor in earth, neither under the earth, was able to open the book, neither to look thereon.**

Void of spiritual perception, man has no mechanism with which to crack the code that binds mankind to sin and death.

4 **And I wept much, because no man was found worthy to open and to read the book, neither to look thereon.**

Giving up all personal ways and means costs us many tears. Physical analysis, human will, ego, pride, imagination, and zeal must be given up in order to read the language of Spirit.

5 **And one of the elders saith unto me, Weep not: behold, the Lion of the tribe of Juda, the Root of David, hath prevailed to open the book, and to loose the seven seals thereof.**

Since no *man* in heaven or on earth or under the earth was able to open the book, the Lion of the tribe of Juda is not a man. Therefore, the root of David was not Jesse, his human father. Omnipotence was the living being that recognized David as regal and identified him in his youth. Christ anointed David and prepared him for the throne as an advocate for good. His Christliness was crude compared to Jesus, but his fearless conviction for good was discernable in song and action, and he received his reward—one like unto him. It is the immediate understanding of Truth, *nous*, which Jesus presents, that prevails to open the book. Jesus lived in the nous. It is neither brainpower nor Spirit that enables one to see, but it is Christ, between the two, that translates Truth to mankind.

In chapter 4, the elders are introduced after the throne and before the sea of glass; thus, the elders are *between* Principle and its idea. Is the elder consciousness, representing king and priest, the *nous* (object of understanding) that opens the book? The power and presence of Christ consciousness occurs at the moment we give up *our* sense of earth and heaven and sit transfixed—with ears to hear.

In the first chapter of Genesis, the divine Us (Elohim) makes perfect man in Our (God's) likeness. This is the correct way to view the Christ and the Christ man, Jesus. He was the first man (Son of man) made and seen as image and likeness and, consequently, the first to demystify (unseal) the book. Without God's idea of man, man cannot identify God.

6 **And I beheld, and, lo, in the midst of the throne and of the four beasts, and in the midst of the elders, stood a Lamb as it had been slain, having seven horns and seven eyes, which are the seven Spirits of God sent forth into all the earth.**

From the center, out of the most holy Principle, and within the deepest consecration of perfect Mind stands the primal quality of being. It is called *Lamb,* and it stands for Love.

Love is the highest, simplest, and most inclusive term for God, and it is the most difficult to comprehend because we cling to our personal sense of love more dearly than anything else. This false love must be slain in order to see the grandeur of God as Love. Jesus Christ bore the dual title of Lamb and Lion, trumpeting the seven horns that sounded the seven messages to contrary humanity. Again, Christ delivers the idea of perfect God and perfect man to earth-based thinkers, consequently lifting them up.

7 **And he came and took the book out of the right hand of him that sat upon the throne.**

The secrets of God are not a handout. The Lamb was worthy and took the initiative. He went and took the book out of the angel's hand, from strength to strength. Jesus set the example for us.

8 **And when he had taken the book, the four beasts and four and twenty elders fell down before the Lamb, having every one of them harps, and golden vials full of odours, which are the prayers of saints.**

The dual quality of the elders reflects the Lamb's slain posture in order to animate their earnest desire—singing praises. Praising God requires great humility, innocence, worthiness, courage of conviction, strength to go forward, and great love. We need tuned harps and ready fingers.

9–10 **And they sung a new song, saying, Thou art worthy to take the book, and to open the seals thereof: for thou wast slain, and hast redeemed us to God by thy blood out of every kindred, and tongue, and people, and nation; And hast made us unto our God kings and priests: and we shall reign on the earth.**

They sang the song of *now* in unison. Humility bows, dominion serves, omnipotence enables, omniscience assures, omnipresence knows, and omni-action delivers.

Christ consciousness fulfills these requirements and stands ready to open the message of the sealed book for each one of us. When we overcome our difficulties, we will rejoice and sing the new song as kings and priests unto God. We will have discovered the joy of life lived by grace.

11–12 **And I beheld, and I heard the voice of many angels round about the throne and the beasts and the elders: and the number of them was ten thousand times ten thousand, and thousands of thousands; Saying with a loud voice, Worthy is the Lamb that was slain to receive power, and riches, and wisdom, and strength, and honour, and glory, and blessing.**

How many assurances do we need of the rightness of Christ? How about one hundred million and millions more waiting in the wings? Be comforted. These angels confirm that Jesus—who manifested the Christ without measure—was bestowed with divine power, riches, wisdom, strength, honor, glory, and love. The Lamb is found worthy to break the seals that enslave mankind.

13 **And every creature which is in heaven, and on the earth, and under the earth, and such as are in the sea, and all that are in them, heard I saying, Blessing, and honour, and glory, and power, be unto him that sitteth upon the throne, and unto the Lamb for ever and ever.**

Christ makes the inevitable obvious, declaring to all that *I Am* is all there is to our being as image and likeness.

14 **And the four beasts said, Amen. And the four and twenty elders fell down and worshipped him that liveth for ever and ever.**

Life just *is*.

UNSEALING THE BOOK

Rev. 6–8:1

Rev. 6

1 And I saw when the Lamb opened **one of the seals**, and
I heard, as it were the noise of thunder,
one of the four beasts saying, *"Come and see."*

2 And I saw, and behold a WHITE HORSE: and he that sat on him had a bow; and a crown was given unto him: and he went forth conquering, and to conquer.

3 And when he had opened the **second seal**, I heard
the second beast say, *"Come and see."*

4 And there went out another HORSE that was RED: and power was given to him that sat thereon to take peace from the earth, and that they should kill one another: and there was given unto him a great sword.

5 And when he had opened the **third seal**, I heard
the third beast say, *"Come and see."*

And I beheld, and lo a BLACK HORSE; and he that
sat on him had a pair of balances in his hand.
6 And I heard a voice in the midst of the four beasts
say,

"A measure of wheat for a penny,
and three measures of barley for a penny;
and see thou hurt not the oil and the wine."

7 And when he had opened the **fourth seal**, I heard the voice
of the fourth beast say, *"Come and see."*

8 And I looked, and behold a PALE HORSE: and his name that sat on him was Death, and Hell followed with him. And Power was given unto them over the

fourth part of the earth, to kill with sword, and with
hunger, and with death, and with the beasts of the
earth.

9 And when he had opened the **fifth seal**, I saw under the
altar the souls of them that were slain for the word of God,
and for the testimony which they held:
10 And they cried with a loud voice, saying,
"How long, O Lord, holy and true, dost thou not judge and
avenge our blood on them that dwell on the earth?"
11 And white robes were given unto every one of them; and it
was said unto them, that they should rest yet for a little
season, until their fellowservants also and their brethren,
that should be killed as they were, should be fulfilled.

12 And I beheld when he had opened the **sixth seal**, and, lo,
there was a great earthquake;
and the sun became black as sackcloth of hair,
and the moon became as blood;
13 And the stars of heaven fell unto the earth, even as a
fig tree casteth her untimely figs, when she is
shaken of a mighty wind.
14 And the heaven departed as a scroll when it is rolled
together;
and every mountain and island were moved out of
their places.

15 And the kings of the earth, and the great men, and the rich
men, and the chief captains, and the mighty men, and every
bondman, and every free man, hid themselves in the dens
and in the rocks of the mountains;
16 And said to the mountains and rocks,
"Fall on us, and hide us from the face of him that sitteth on
the throne, and from the wrath of the Lamb:
17 For the great day of his wrath is come;
and who shall be able to stand?"

Rev. 7

1 And after these things I saw

FOUR ANGELS STANDING ON THE FOUR CORNERS OF THE EARTH,
holding the four winds of the earth,
that the wind should not blow on the earth,
nor on the sea, nor on any tree.

2 And I saw another angel ascending from the east, having
the seal of the living God: and he cried with a loud voice to
the four angels, to whom it was given to hurt the earth and
the sea,
3 Saying,

"Hurt not the earth, neither the sea, nor the trees, till we have sealed the servants of our God in their foreheads."

4 And I heard the number of them which were sealed: and
there were sealed an hundred and forty and four thousand
of all the tribes of the children of Israel.

5 Of the tribe of Juda were sealed twelve thousand.
Of the tribe of Reuben were sealed twelve thousand.
Of the tribe of Gad were sealed twelve thousand.
6 Of the tribe of Aser were sealed twelve thousand.
Of the tribe of Nephthalim were sealed twelve thousand.
Of the tribe of Manasses were sealed twelve thousand.
7 Of the tribe of Simeon were sealed twelve thousand.
Of the tribe of Levi were sealed twelve thousand.
Of the tribe of Issachar were sealed twelve thousand.
8 Of the tribe of Zabulon were sealed twelve thousand.
Of the tribe of Joseph were sealed twelve thousand.
Of the tribe of Benjamin were sealed twelve thousand.

9 After this I beheld, and, lo, a great multitude, which no man
could number, of all nations, and kindreds, and people, and

tongues, stood before the throne, and before the Lamb, clothed with white robes, and palms in their hands;
10 And cried with a loud voice, saying, "Salvation to our God which sitteth upon the throne, and unto the Lamb."

11 And all the angels stood round about the throne, and about the elders and the four beasts, and fell before the throne on their faces, and worshipped God,
12 Saying,

"Amen: Blessing, and glory, and wisdom, and thanksgiving, and honour, and power, and might, be unto our God for ever and ever. Amen."

13 And one of the elders answered, saying unto me, "What are these which are arrayed in white robes? and whence came they?"
14 And I said unto him, "Sir, thou knowest." And he said to me, "These are they which came out of great tribulation, and have washed their robes, and made them white in the blood of the Lamb."
15 Therefore are they before the throne of God, and serve him day and night in his temple: and

he that sitteth on the throne shall dwell among them.

16 They shall hunger no more, neither thirst any more; neither shall the sun light on them, nor any heat.
17 For the Lamb which is in the midst of the throne shall feed them, and shall lead them unto living fountains of waters: and
God shall wipe away all tears from their eyes.

Rev. 8

1 And when he had opened the **seventh seal**, there was

SILENCE IN HEAVEN
about the space of half an hour.

Unsealing the Book

Rev. 6–8:1

The evil that blocks our comprehension of the Word is exposed as the seals are opened one by one. Each seal represents a particular fault in human nature: the first four reveal the errors that hide our royal inheritance, and the last three reveal the hatred of Truth that inhibits priesthood. Evil must be seen for what it is and for what it is not before spiritual progress can be made.

Rev. 6

1 **And I saw when the Lamb opened one of the seals, and I heard, as it were the noise of thunder, one of the four beasts saying, Come and see.**

Enthroned in the seat of power, the Lamb breaks the primary seal that binds man: the belief in a power opposed to God. Omnipotence sends forth a resounding call to John: 'Come, sit with the Lamb and watch this vain attempt of man to take power into his own hands. The book is locked up tight to him. He is clueless!'

2 **And I saw, and behold a white horse: and he that sat on him had a bow; and a crown was given unto him: and he went forth conquering, and to conquer.**

As newborn egos conceived in sin, our first desire is to conquer the world and rule over it, like a self-crowned prince on a white horse. Mankind repeats Satan's line: "I will be like the most High" (Isa. 14:14). Egotism, self-will, animal courage, enthusiasm, humanism, and confidence in physical sense and material law make us blind to our real origin as sons and daughters of God. Egotism sees nothing but itself; the book is completely sealed.

3 **And when he had opened the second seal, I heard the second beast say, Come and see.**

The Lamb and John are sharing a serene sense of God's omniscience, when John hears, in substance, 'Come and see what happens when humanity encounters many minds. They are ignorant of Mind as One. Can you imagine not knowing how to love one another? Look at them. They are surface dwellers who read the Word, hear it literally, and then find fault with *Me*.'

4 **And there went out another horse that was red: and power was given to him that sat thereon to take peace from the earth, and that they should kill one another: and there was given unto him a great sword.**

The *rage* of egotism desires to crush all other egos, thus creating perpetual warfare. Murder is self-justified. Cain, arguing with the Lord, asked, "Am I my brother's keeper?" (Gen. 4:9). Unaware of anything spiritual and seduced by the belief in human evolution that insists on *survival of the fittest*, man attempts to push all others down in order to exalt himself. Envy, jealousy, covetousness, betrayal, cheating, and lying allow nothing more than a superficial reading of the book, and self-justification is the first to blame God for not explaining it better.

5… **And when he had opened the third seal, I heard the third beast say, Come and see.**

John and the Lamb are in the light together. Through the omnipresent Spirit, John hears, in essence, 'Watch with me. Do you see what happens when man attempts to gain substance on his own? It's obvious why it doesn't work—pathetic even. He doesn't know that there's nothing there to gain. Didn't he hear when I said, "Judge not, that ye be not judged"? (Matt. 7:1). They will use the book to judge me (Jesus) and fight against Me (God).'

…5–6 **And I beheld, and lo a black horse; and he that sat on him had a pair of balances in his hand. And I heard a voice in the midst of the four beasts say, A measure of wheat for a penny, and three measures of barley for a penny; and see thou hurt not the oil and the wine.**

Comparisons and so-called *free choice* lead downward, away from the light, toward total darkness. Where it is *black*, nothing grows. The result is famine, poverty, and the complete loss of enlightenment. "A measure of wheat for a penny" is starvation wages, barely enough to buy a day's worth of grain for one person. It leaves nothing available to share. "Hurt not the oil and the wine" is a warning not to forget that consecration to good (oil) and the inspiration of divine justice (wine) are ever with us, and we can avail ourselves of these resources if we can be still enough to hear them.

Judging one another, finding fault, and acting self-righteously tramples prophecy, avoids consecration, and blocks inspiration. Black-horse mentality would use the sealed book in an evil way to suit its own purpose, blinding others with false pontifications. The Master declared, "I can of mine own self do nothing: as I hear, I judge: and my judgment is just; because I seek not mine own will, but the will of the Father which hath sent me" (John 5:30). When Christ judges, omnipresence is on one side of the scale, and nothing is on the other side. As we love one another, expecting nothing in return except what Love has to offer, we gain the light divine and one another.

7 **And when he had opened the fourth seal, I heard the voice of the fourth beast say, Come and see.**

The Lamb's activity knows no bounds because Christ is not confined within a finite universe. As John becomes enlivened by the nature and character of God as omni-action, he is prepared to witness the Lamb's work.

'Come and see the sad result of mortals believing in a finite universe where they are born and die. From where we sit, are there any limitations?'

8 **And I looked, and behold a pale horse: and his name that sat on him was Death, and Hell followed with him. And Power was given unto them over the fourth part of the earth, to kill with sword, and with hunger, and with death, and with the beasts of the earth.**

The "valley of the shadow of death" (Ps. 23:4) haunts us from the cradle to the grave. It is this fear of inevitable failure that makes us hesitate, act shy, feel pale, faint, become discouraged, give up, age, or attempt suicide.

We might memorize the content of the book, yet we fail to pursue it to any logical conclusion. Doubt leaves the book unread.

9–11 **And when he had opened the fifth seal, I saw under the altar the souls of them that were slain for the word of God, and for the testimony which they held: And they cried with a loud voice, saying, How long, O Lord, holy and true, dost thou not judge and avenge our blood on them that dwell on the earth? And white robes were given unto every one of them; and it was said unto them, that they should rest yet for a little season, until their fellowservants also and their brethren, that should be killed as they were, should be fulfilled.**

One cannot be *under* the altar without having once been placed *on* the altar where lambs are baptized by fire. The heart, once purified, finds success in holiness where the old domineering mind had failed. Feeling stuck under the altar and waiting for consolation from heaven can only occur when one entertains a finite sense of the infinite. Jesus overcame the world. Ultimately, every one of us must be baptized and find himself under the altar. When everyone is there, so is heaven, and the finite sense is dissolved.

The instinct to persecute the righteous, to mock those whose purity makes us feel uncomfortable, is *malice*. The belief of the finite needs to be forgotten and the malice of hatred erased.

> Blessed are they which are persecuted for righteousness' sake: for theirs is the kingdom of heaven (Matt. 5:10).

12–13 **And I beheld when he had opened the sixth seal, and, lo, there was a great earthquake; and the sun became black as sackcloth of hair, and the moon became as blood; And the stars of heaven fell unto the earth, even as a fig tree casteth her untimely figs, when she is shaken of a mighty wind.**

The dawning of truth is a great shock to the self-absorbed, who are lost in the confines of a material universe. When we realize the hopelessness and vanity of sin, our world collapses into utter despair. We struggle long and hard to regain our position, clinging to our *earthly belongings*. But Truth continues knocking at the door of our conscience, making us feel guilty.

14 **And the heaven departed as a scroll when it is rolled together; and every mountain and island were moved out of their places.**

The inevitable demand of truth shocks the very foundations of everything that we have been taught to believe. It is too much to bear!

15–16 **And the kings of the earth, and the great men, and the rich men, and the chief captains, and the mighty men, and every bondman, and every free man, hid themselves in the dens and in the rocks of the mountains; And said to the mountains and rocks, Fall on us, and hide us from the face of him that sitteth on the throne, and from the wrath of the Lamb:**

All ego-driven personalities run for cover as if screaming in retreat: 'Hide us at all cost! This innocence has taken away all the tricks of our trade, all our contrivances, and all our playtime; it has made our guilt obvious.'

17 **For the great day of his wrath is come; and who shall be able to stand?**

We hear it exclaimed, 'Oh, my God! I've done everything wrong! Nobody can live up to these standards.' When we see the terrible mistake of living life falsely, living the charade and taunting righteousness, we see no way out and think it impossible to achieve mastery over our own sin. Judas, after he saw what he had done, tried to hide behind suicide.

> And then shall appear the sign of the Son of man in heaven: and then shall all the tribes of the earth mourn (Matt. 24:30).

Rev. 7

However dreadful it seems, the hopelessness and terror occasioned by exposed sin provides an opportunity for enlightenment. Prophetic reassurances are offered in chapter 7 to encourage man to push on to his ultimate glory.

1 **And after these things I saw four angels standing on the four corners of the earth, holding the four winds of the earth, that the wind should not blow on the earth, nor on the sea, nor on any tree.**

The passions that were once swirling about—making us busy, intoxicated, or complacent—have now been stilled. We are ready to consider a profound thought.

> And he shall send his angels with a great sound of a trumpet, and they shall gather together his elect from the four winds, from one end of heaven to the other (Matt. 24:31).

He leadeth me beside the still waters (Ps. 23:2).

2–3 **And I saw another angel ascending from the east, having the seal of the living God: and he cried with a loud voice to the four angels, to whom it was given to hurt the earth and the sea, Saying, Hurt not the earth, neither the sea, nor the trees, till we have sealed the servants of our God in their foreheads.**

Be assured that universal salvation will come, but first goodness must be understood and empower man's life with grace. Then man will not mind being still; he will desire it. Individually and collectively, our names are already written in heaven. It is time for us to know it.

4 **And I heard the number of them which were sealed: and there were sealed an hundred and forty and four thousand of all the tribes of the children of Israel.**

Everyone who has the Ten Commandments written in his forehead is a child of Israel: conscience persists in telling us what not to do. Regardless of human ancestry, class distinction, or circumstance, as soon as we are obedient to the divine impulse, we feel the satisfaction of being on the right path. We are all on the list.

5 **Of the tribe of Juda were sealed twelve thousand.**
Of the tribe of Reuben were sealed twelve thousand.
Of the tribe of Gad were sealed twelve thousand.
6 **Of the tribe of Aser were sealed twelve thousand.**
Of the tribe of Nephthalim were sealed twelve thousand.
Of the tribe of Manasses were sealed twelve thousand.
7 **Of the tribe of Simeon were sealed twelve thousand.**
Of the tribe of Levi were sealed twelve thousand.
Of the tribe of Issachar were sealed twelve thousand.
8 **Of the tribe of Zabulon were sealed twelve thousand.**
Of the tribe of Joseph were sealed twelve thousand.
Of the tribe of Benjamin were sealed twelve thousand.

9–10 **After this I beheld, and, lo, a great multitude, which no man could number, of all nations, and kindreds, and people, and tongues, stood before the throne, and before the Lamb, clothed with white robes, and palms in their hands; And cried with a loud voice, saying, Salvation to our God which sitteth upon the throne, and unto the Lamb.**

The name of each child of Israel has a spiritual meaning and divine purpose that must be realized: Juda, praise of God; Reuben, son of vision; Gad, company prepared; Aser, happy; Nephthalim, wrestling to see God; Manasses, he made to forget; Simeon, gracious hearing; Levi, my joining; Issachar, he brings a reward; Zabulon, abiding habitation; Joseph, to perfect; and Benjamin, son of my right hand. Each tribe represents a type of human experience that is overcome through Christ. The man of God's creating is identified, present, sealed, and rejoicing.

11–12 **And all the angels stood round about the throne, and about the elders and the four beasts, and fell before the throne on their faces, and worshipped God, Saying, Amen: Blessing, and glory, and wisdom, and thanksgiving, and honour, and power, and might, be unto our God for ever and ever. Amen.**

Everything from mental microbe to infinite idea joins the victory chorus in one grand theme of holy gratitude. There is no stopping them.

13–14 **And one of the elders answered, saying unto me, What are these which are arrayed in white robes? and whence came they? And I said unto him, Sir, thou knowest.**

Humble John stood, a master of Mind's manifestation, knowing all but opening not his mouth. He knew that "the Word was with God, and the Word was God" (John 1:1). Out of supreme stillness, all answers arrive spontaneously without any effort on our part.

14–17 **And he said to me, These are they which came out of great tribulation, and have washed their robes, and made them white in the blood of the Lamb. Therefore are they before the throne of God, and serve him day and night in his temple: and he that sitteth on the throne shall dwell among them. They shall hunger no more, neither thirst any more; neither shall the sun light on them, nor any heat. For the Lamb which is in the midst of the throne shall feed them, and shall lead them unto living fountains of waters: and God shall wipe away all tears from their eyes.**

Christ's mission is fully realized. Everything that *we* have ever *thought,* was wrong; everything that God *knows,* is right. God is self-generating Life and joy, and we are that life joyfully lived!

Rev. 8
With all this prophecy about to be fulfilled, here is the last woe—the final test and triumph for humanity.

1 **And when he had opened the seventh seal, there was silence in heaven about the space of half an hour.**

> Be silent, O all flesh, before the Lord: for he is raised up out of his holy habitation (Zech. 2:13).

Why is silence a woe? Silence is difficult. It is absolutely essential to know how to be unfazed by the torrents of mortal mind. The prophets of old gained their victories by finding silence in the midst of their woes: John sang hymns of praise while drenched in a pot of boiling oil, the three Hebrew men walked comfortably in the burning fiery furnace, and Daniel felt safe in the lion's den. They rose above the clamoring senses, silent and alive. Jesus sustained silence for three days in the tomb. Also, during his three-and-a-half-year ministry, Jesus could not tell his disciples all that he knew. He patiently waited for the Holy Ghost to descend upon them, and then he rejoiced because he knew they were being fed directly from the source.

We all must taste this experience and feel the incredible peace that comes from being wrapped up in Love. The world will scream at us to conform to physical evidence and die, but we will be so focused on the thoughts of Mind that we will not even notice.

SEVEN ANGELS SOUND—BAPTISM BY FIRE

Rev. 8:2–9:21 (Angels 1–6)

Rev. 8

2 And I saw the **seven angels which stood before God**; and to them were given **seven trumpets.**

3 And **another angel came and stood at the altar, having a golden censer**; and there was given unto him much incense, that he should offer it with the prayers of all saints upon the golden altar which was before the throne.
4 And the smoke of the incense, which came with the prayers of the saints, ascended up before God out of the angel's hand.
5 **And the angel took the censer, and filled it with fire of the altar, and cast it into the earth:** and there were voices, and thunderings, and lightnings, and an earthquake.

6 And the seven angels which had the seven trumpets prepared themselves to sound.

7 The **first angel sounded**, and there followed hail and fire mingled with blood, and they were cast upon the earth: and
the third part of **trees was burnt up**,
and all **green grass was burnt up**.

8 And the **second angel sounded**, and as it were a great mountain burning with fire was cast into the sea: and the
third part of the **sea became blood**;
9 And the third part of the **creatures** which were in the sea, and had life, **died**;
and the third part of the **ships were destroyed**.

10 And the **third angel sounded**, and there fell a great star from heaven, burning as it were a lamp, and it fell upon the third part of the **rivers**, and upon the fountains of waters;

11 And the name of the star is called **Wormwood**: and the
third part of the **waters became wormwood**; and many
men died of the waters, because they were made **bitter**.

12 And the **fourth angel sounded**, and
the third part of the **sun was smitten**,
and the third part of the **moon**,
and the third part of the **stars**; so as the third part of
them was **darkened**,
and the **day shone not** for a third part of it, and the
night likewise.

13 And I beheld, and heard an angel flying through the midst
of heaven, saying with a loud voice, "WOE, WOE, WOE,
to the inhabiters of the earth by reason of the other voices
of the trumpet of the three angels, which are yet to sound!"

Rev. 9

1 And the **fifth angel sounded**, and I saw a star fall from
heaven unto the earth: and to him was given the **key of the
bottomless pit**.

2 And he opened the bottomless pit; and there arose a
smoke out of the pit, as the smoke of a great
furnace; and the sun and the air were darkened by
reason of the smoke of the pit.

3 And there came out of the smoke **locusts** upon the
earth: and unto them was given power, as the
scorpions of the earth have power.

4 And it was commanded them that they should not
hurt the grass of the earth, neither any green thing,
neither any tree; but **only those men which have
not the seal of God in their foreheads.**

5 And to them it was given that they should not kill
them, but that they should be **tormented five
months**: and their torment was as the torment of a
scorpion, when he striketh a man.

6 And in those days shall men seek death, and shall
not find it; and shall desire to die, and **death shall
flee from them.**

7 And the shapes of the **locusts** were **like unto horses**
prepared unto battle; and on their heads were as it
were **crowns like gold**, and their faces were as the
faces of men.
8 And they had hair as the **hair of women**, and their
teeth were as the **teeth of lions**.
9 And they had breastplates, as it were **breastplates**
of iron; and the sound of their wings was as the
sound of chariots of many horses running to battle.
10 And they had **tails like unto scorpions**, and there
were stings in their tails: and their power was to
hurt men five months.

11 And they had a **king over them**, which is the angel
of the bottomless pit, whose name in the Hebrew
tongue is **Abaddon**, but in the Greek tongue hath
his name **Apollyon**.

12 ONE WOE is past; and, behold, there come TWO WOES
more hereafter.

13 And the **sixth angel sounded**, and I heard a voice from the
four horns of the golden altar which is before God,
14 Saying to the sixth angel which had the trumpet,

"Loose the four angels which are bound
in the great river Euphrates."

15 And the four angels were loosed, which were
prepared for an hour, and a day, and a month, and a
year, for to slay the third part of men.

16 And the number of the army of the horsemen were
two hundred thousand thousand: and I heard the
number of them.

17 And thus I saw the horses in the vision, and them
that sat on them, having breastplates of FIRE, and
of JACINTH, and BRIMSTONE: and the heads of
the horses were as the heads of lions; and out of
their mouths issued fire and smoke and brimstone.

18 By these three was the third part of men killed, by
the FIRE, and by the SMOKE, and by the
BRIMSTONE, which issued out of their mouths.
19 For their power is in their mouth, and in their tails:
for their tails were like unto serpents, and had
heads, and with them they do hurt.

20 And the rest of the men which were not killed by these
plagues yet repented not of the works of their hands, that
they should not worship devils, and idols of gold, and
silver, and brass, and stone, and of wood: which neither can
see, nor hear, nor walk:
21 Neither repented they of their murders, nor of their
sorceries, nor of their fornication, nor of their thefts.

Seven Angels Sound—Baptism by Fire
View from the Altar

Rev. 8:2–9:21 (Angels 1–6) and Rev. 11:14–19 (Angel 7)
In the opening of the seven seals, we saw how man's depravity prevents access to a present knowledge of God until the "four angels standing on the four corners of the earth" hold the winds of the earth still for examination. Now the sounding of seven angels records the effects of this examination, separating man from the beast by fire. The examination begins on the outer surface of material things, with the first angel, and progressively probes deeper and deeper into the errors that mortal man is making in defense of his so-called existence.

To the self-justified and unenlightened beast man, it is easier for him to either plead ignorance of Revelation or to mock it than it is for him to remove the errors that feed his attachment to the mortal body and mind. Indulging in sin, however, has its penalties, and sooner or later the pleasure recedes and man begins to suffer from either regret or pain. This suffering, which ultimately separates us from sin, is *baptism by fire from the altar.* The seven angels strip away our coverings one by one, revealing how we have been fooled.

It is interesting to note that the actual *sounding* messages of the angels are not recorded, yet their potency is apparent by the dramatic effect they have on mortal man and his surroundings. In each case, as an angel sounds, the one on the altar loses some thing or error that is blocking recognition of his spiritual identity. Not until the presentation of the last WOE at the end of chapter 11 do we hear what is being said in heaven as a grand response to the seventh angel.

In chapter 8, as a result of the first four angels sounding, the lie that makes man believe himself to be derived from and operating in a material universe is exposed and destroyed. In rapid succession, the physical body, the theory of evolution from the sea, organic chemistry, and the physics of the material universe fall before the light of Truth.

In chapter 9, the fifth and the sixth angels initiate two great WOES. At the end of chapter 11, the seventh angel propagates a concluding WOE. These last three angel messengers cause us to plunge beneath the surface of *things* to expose the hidden mental process by which we are fooled, to point out how mortal mind lies, and to prophesy evil's ultimate destruction.

As we have seen before, the *sixth* stage provides the spiritual solution for the remaining stage and for all the previous stages in the human experience. Love is providing the spiritual assurance and understanding that is necessary to finish the work. Chapters 10 and 11 prophesy the glorious means by which the cleansing is to be completed and the victory won.

The exaggerated views from the altar are not distorted pictures of truth or error; rather, they describe the unpleasant reaction that occurs when Truth exposes error, bringing light into the darkness. Depending on our point of view, we are either horrified and in sympathy with suffering man, or we are like scientific observers in a laboratory, watching a chemical reaction between two opposing fluids. The scientific observer has the better view.

Rev. 8

2 **And I saw the seven angels which stood before God; and to them were given seven trumpets.**

Infinite Christ stands ready to communicate with mortal man, and all divine resources are available and at hand.

3 **And another angel came and stood at the altar, having a golden censer; and there was given unto him much**

incense, that he should offer it with the prayers of all saints upon the golden altar which was before the throne.

Life's aroma permeates every quality and condition of thought with priceless assurance. Christ's mission—to free mankind from the slavery of his own self-interest—stands ready to inspire every waking thought, and every prayer offered in response to Christ magnifies that mission.

4–5… **And the smoke of the incense, which came with the prayers of the saints, ascended up before God out of the angel's hand. And the angel took the censer, and filled it with fire of the altar, and cast it into the earth:**

Spiritual vision requires spiritual insight, and that vision is always reflected back to its origin, God. The best of humanity reflects Christ's idea to some extent and knows it, but a filthy mind is clueless. Regardless of the thoughts that we are entertaining at the moment, Christ demands that perfect man be seen as perfect reflection and aids this recognition by doing a thorough cleansing of each one of us. To those who are either ignorant of this process or clinging to the dirt in defiance of Christ, it is hellfire. When we are ready to give up *our way* for the divine—when we lay our earthly all upon the altar and anticipate the promised purity—all fear dissolves, and we discover that we will lose nothing.

…5 **and there were voices, and thunderings, and lightnings, and an earthquake.**

The pattern of the seven angelic voices is as follows:

- First, Mind *voices*, 'I Am.'
- Second, the *thunder* of error complains itself away.
- Third, error is seen as mere illusive *lightning*.
- Fourth, the human mind is shaken like an *earthquake* to a change of base.

True to apocalyptic practice, the first shall be last, and the last shall be first. Our sense sees this unfolding sequence in reverse order from the divine directive:

- First, the earthly minded feel a great temporal stir like an *earthquake*.
- Second, Satan falls from heaven as *lightning*—sin is knocked off its base and is no longer worshipped.
- Third, arrogance *thunders* error's demise and fades into oblivion.
- Fourth, the *voice* of truth is heard and understood.

6 **And the seven angels which had the seven trumpets prepared themselves to sound.**

Truth is always ready.

7 **The first angel sounded, and there followed hail and fire mingled with blood, and they were cast upon the earth: and the third part of trees was burnt up, and all green grass was burnt up.**

Angel messengers that stand before God are filled with God's goodness, incapable of inflicting evil or pain. The first angel is not bringing a plague but is shining a light, making us aware that we are plagued by sorrowful illusions. We are forced to examine our attachment to the outer surface of self (our physical body) and to witness its destruction as an apparent reality.

> I am come to send fire on the earth; and what will I, if it be already kindled? But I have a baptism to be baptized with; and how am I straitened till it be accomplished! Suppose ye that I am come to give peace on earth? I tell you, Nay; but rather division (Luke 12:49–51).

> And if a house be divided against itself, that house cannot stand (Mark 3:25).

Infinity can neither be divided nor burned, but anything that is finite is subject to destruction; therefore, finite things are unlike God. Baptism by fire makes this distinction obvious to struggling humanity. If we are physically thrown into a fire, the first and most obvious sensation is the pain of burning flesh. The blaze of Truth begins to remove the surface trappings of humanity's home.

The term *earth* as used here is not something external to us; *we* are the earthly subjects on the altar. Truth is attacking our sense of self as a finite physical body with physical surroundings and dependency. Our body, which is our mental home, is a city of passions entertained through the physical senses. Once the identity attached to a physical body is destroyed, green herbs provided for man's use are no longer palatable or available in the literal sense.

The term *one-third* symbolizes that which has no part in God because God is indivisible. From our vantage point, there appears to be three phases of existence: heavenly, earthly, and heavenly again. Only a third part—man's earthly concept of himself—can be destroyed.

8 **And the second angel sounded, and as it were a great mountain burning with fire was cast into the sea: and the third part of the sea became blood;**

The result of the second angel sounding causes us to follow the trail of material body back to its so-called origin in the sea. Mortal man's conviction that he evolved from sea slime is reduced to its primal element, blood, for examination. Blood is essentially seawater, which has no inherent life in its elemental composition.

9 **And the third part of the creatures which were in the sea, and had life, died; and the third part of the ships were destroyed.**

Metaphorically, the salt sea has lost its savor. We are forced to admit that nothing of value can be derived from slime or genetics to explain our real existence. Our belief in a sea origin never had the vital properties essential for life as God manifest.

10 **And the third angel sounded, and there fell a great star from heaven, burning as it were a lamp, and it fell upon the third part of the rivers, and upon the fountains of waters;**

The effect of the third trumpet greatly intensifies the search, forcing us to look further upstream at the cause and effect of believing that a water origin is capable of producing building blocks of life. Stripped of genetics as a basis for life, all functions tributary to it must be seriously called into question and scrutinized. With no source of life in the chemicals that build complex genetic codes, nothing can effectively evolve or live.

11 **And the name of the star is called Wormwood: and the third part of the waters became wormwood; and many men died of the waters, because they were made bitter.**

Biological phenomena that was once thought to accurately describe the most basic life processes is found full of holes. Whole fields of study that were previously assumed to be scientific are no longer tenable. The enlightened human mind, finding earth-based functions useless, must either suffer the bitter sense of defeat that the death of these errors brings or it must trace all life back to God by studying the perfect Christ model, which Jesus presented.

12 **And the fourth angel sounded, and the third part of the sun was smitten, and the third part of the moon, and the third part of the stars; so as the third part of them was darkened, and the day shone not for a third part of it, and the night likewise.**

The effect of the fourth angel destroys the credibility of the physical universe and its laws. All earth-based laws are hung on the framework of the cosmos. Christ systematically strips away all physical structure that we assume is essential for life. We cannot build on anything here to substantiate life, not even physics.

13 **And I beheld, and heard an angel flying through the midst of heaven, saying with a loud voice, Woe, woe, woe, to the inhabiters of the earth by reason of the other voices of the trumpet of the three angels, which are yet to sound!**

The messenger, flying high above physical phenomena, sees right through the guise of the mysteriously evolved beast and prepares to expose the root of error. If you think that looking at the outside effects is shocking, wait until you see what is causing all these disturbances!

Rev. 9

The fifth angel causes the many facades of the belief in a power opposed to God to be examined. The sixth angel exposes that which would attempt to mystify Christ. Each woe magnifies the previous one by looking more deeply and shining the light more brightly. Christ is lighting up like a star, a mental microscope to show us the inner impulses that animate body and titillate the senses.

1 **And the fifth angel sounded, and I saw a star fall from heaven unto the earth: and to him was given the key of the bottomless pit.**

If we are convinced of the illusive nature of matter by using the human intellect—deciphering material law with brainpower—how can we use that same brainpower to decipher itself? It simply cannot be done. We have reached the limits of human conception. However, Christ is not animated by brainpower, and the light of Truth can certainly solve the riddle. Christ has the key to the bottomless pit and will use that key to expose the secret errors that trouble humanity, emptying our mental vessels of their filth so that they may be filled with the spiritual definitions of Life and Love.

2 **And he opened the bottomless pit; and there arose a smoke out of the pit, as the smoke of a great furnace; and the sun and the air were darkened by reason of the smoke of the pit.**

Metaphorically, the bottomless pit defines itself by what is not seen and by how it controls mortals within its influence. The bottomless pit is the antithesis of the infinite. It is like a black hole controlling everything within its magnetic range, compressing its subjects into ever smaller and smaller orbits, unable to radiate light out upon the universe. Resisting examination and diverting attention with a veil of smoke, it is stubborn, dark, mysterious, polluted, self-consuming, and scorching hot. The bottomless pit would discourage the pursuit of error's secrets through fear of torment and threats of persecution.

3 **And there came out of the smoke locusts upon the earth: and unto them was given power, as the scorpions of the earth have power.**

Mortal mind is screaming not to be found out, and it will attempt to overwhelm the investigator with a torrent of fears. These are the fears that cling to us, even as we cling to them.

4 **And it was commanded them that they should not hurt the grass of the earth, neither any green thing, neither any tree, but only those men which have not the seal of God in their foreheads.**

Grass, green things, and trees have nothing to dread because they have no conscience and, therefore, cannot sin. This is war in one's forehead; there is no external event, object, circumstance, or offense to justify the fear. The battle must be waged in the thought that sins, and the error must be expunged through knowledge of salvation and by the very pain the sin brings.

5 **And to them it was given that they should not kill them, but that they should be tormented five months: and their torment was as the torment of a scorpion, when he striketh a man.**

Error has no power at all to kill Truth, but the five senses lie and, therefore, are subject to attack, torture, and total loss. Ignorant of spiritual sense, the thought of losing one's senses is more than the mind is willing to tolerate. So Christ comes to where we are and teaches with the very tools we have provided. Since nerve is the faculty that transmits feeling, Christ reaches out by declaring the truth that initiates self-guilt, subsequently making nerve sting.

6 **And in those days shall men seek death, and shall not find it; and shall desire to die, and death shall flee from them.**

Mortal man would rather be dead than admit his Father to be Spirit; nonetheless, mortal life is powerless to affect Life one way or the other since it has none in reality.

7 **And the shapes of the locusts were like unto horses prepared unto battle; and on their heads were as it were crowns like gold, and their faces were as the faces of men.**

A multitude of suggestions disguised as our own thoughts consume every waking moment with promises of pleasure, threats, fears, and illusions of grandeur. The generator of suggestion—evil, Satan, or mortal mind—was never pretty, yet we accommodate it for its entertainment value and make excuses for our shortcomings.

8–9 **And they had hair as the hair of women, and their teeth were as the teeth of lions. And they had breastplates, as it were breastplates of iron; and the sound of their wings was as the sound of chariots of many horses running to battle.**

Lustful vanity justifies its self-indulgent behavior, flashing its consumer teeth in defiance of truth. Fortified with an ironclad heart, it goes roaring about on flights of fancy, hoping someone will notice.

10 **And they had tails like unto scorpions, and there were stings in their tails: and their power was to hurt men five months.**

Mortal mind reigns over the five physical senses. The ultimate weapon, pain in every form and in every sense, lashes out to enforce obedience: ugliness teases the eyes, dissonance annoys the ears, bitterness threatens the tongue, pain cramps the muscle, and stench violates the nostrils.

11 **And they had a king over them, which is the angel of the bottomless pit, whose name in the Hebrew tongue is Abaddon, but in the Greek tongue hath his name Apollyon.**

Destruction is the motive-power that rules the bottomless pit. From birth to death, mortal man, left to his own devices, can reach no higher and sink no deeper than ground zero.

12 **One woe is past; and, behold, there come two woes more hereafter.**

Mortal mind is the monster of mortal man, and the first prospects of overcoming that influence appear bleak. So Christ delivers more evidence.

13–14 **And the sixth angel sounded, and I heard a voice from the four horns of the golden altar which is before God, Saying to the sixth angel which had the trumpet, Loose the four angels which are bound in the great river Euphrates.**

Good, in all its forms, trumpets a call to understand reality, which is all that is left after our fiery baptism on the altar. Instilled with spiritual potential to deliver its mighty message to desperate humanity, Euphrates encompasses, embraces, and distributes the Word.

15 **And the four angels were loosed, which were prepared for an hour, and a day, and a month, and a year, for to slay the third part of men.**

The same four angels that were seen holding the four winds of the earth in Revelation 7:1 are now prepared for active duty by the four horns of the golden altar. (They were restrained until the servants of God could be sealed in their foreheads.) The structure of Truth and Love, in this and every moment, unseats *destruction* and slays the picture called mortal man, but not God's image. When Jesus walked forth from the grave, was he not emphatically declaring, 'Death is dead. Killing the material body cannot destroy Life. I am still here'?

16 **And the number of the army of the horsemen were two hundred thousand thousand: and I heard the number of them.**

Truths, two hundred million strong, will overwhelm every element of the lie.

17–19 **And thus I saw the horses in the vision, and them that sat on them, having breastplates of fire, and of jacinth, and brimstone: and the heads of the horses were as the heads of lions; and out of their mouths issued fire and smoke and brimstone. By these three was the third part of men killed, by the fire, and by the smoke, and by the brimstone, which issued out of their mouths. For their power is in their mouth, and in their tails: for their tails were like unto serpents, and had heads, and with them they do hurt.**

The fire from the altar of Truth, the stench of exposed sin, and the authority of divine illumination witness the fall of mortal man, stung to death by his own acknowledged mistake. This evil-impregnated man has been duped by addictive brainwaves to inflict his own pain, confusion, and terror. "WOE is me!" (Isa. 6:5).

20–21 **And the rest of the men which were not killed by these plagues yet repented not of the works of their hands, that they should not worship devils, and idols of gold, and silver, and brass, and stone, and of wood: which neither can see, nor hear, nor walk: Neither repented they of their murders, nor of their sorceries, nor of their fornication, nor of their thefts.**

Unrepentant error clings relentlessly to its own gods until God as Love explains Truth through a LITTLE BOOK OPEN and a REED LIKE A ROD. Then individualized man defeats his sense of an enemy.

A LITTLE BOOK OPEN

Rev. 10

1 And I saw another mighty angel come down from heaven,
clothed with a cloud: and
a rainbow was upon his head, and
his face was as it were the sun, and
his feet as pillars of fire:

2 And he had in his hand

A LITTLE BOOK OPEN

and he set his right foot upon the sea,
and his left foot on the earth,

3 And cried with a loud voice, as when a lion roareth: and
when he had cried, **seven thunders uttered their voices.**
4 And when the seven thunders had uttered their voices,
I was about to write: and I heard a voice from heaven
saying unto me,
**"Seal up those things which the seven thunders uttered,
and write them not."**

5 And the angel which I saw stand upon the sea and upon the
earth lifted up his hand to heaven,
6 And sware by him that liveth for ever and ever, who
created heaven, and the things that therein are, and the
earth, and the things that therein are, and the sea, and the
things which are therein, that there should be

TIME NO LONGER:

7 But in the days of the voice of the seventh angel, when he
shall begin to sound,

THE MYSTERY OF GOD SHOULD BE FINISHED,

as he hath declared to his servants the prophets.

8 And the voice which I heard from heaven spake unto me
again, and said,

"Go and take the little book which is open
in the hand of the angel which standeth
upon the sea and upon the earth."

9 And I went unto the angel, and said unto him,

"Give me the little book."

And he said unto me,

"Take it, and eat it up;
and it shall make thy belly bitter,
but it shall be in thy mouth sweet as honey."

10 And I took the little book out of the angel's hand, and ate it
up; and it was in my mouth sweet as honey: and as soon as
I had eaten it, my belly was bitter.

11 And he said unto me,

"Thou must prophesy again before many peoples,
and nations, and tongues, and kings."

Preface to A LITTLE BOOK OPEN

If we have been listening carefully to the angel messages in the previous visions, following the logic, and doing our own work faithfully, we are prepared and will receive the little book open. Before we proceed with this transformational awakening, below is a brief outline of where we have been and what we are about to accomplish.

If we have

1. remembered our first love, Light;
2. held to the First Commandment through fiery trials;
3. learned to discern between the finite and the infinite;
4. stopped trying to have religion in our head, hypocrisy;
5. become consecrated;
6. learned that Love is the KEY;
7. overcome lethargy toward knowing God,

Messages to the Churches Rev. 2,3

deciphered the symbols that identify God, and

The Throne Rev. 4

bonded with Christ presence and accepted his correction;

The Sealed Book Rev. 5

then we have given up

1. our egotism,
2. our envy,
3. our false judgment,
4. our pallid lack of faith,
5. our hatred of Christ, and
6. all efforts to save ourselves by hiding behind a veil,
7. **and we have learned to be STILL.**

Unsealing The Book Rev. 6–8:1

At this point, we are willing to be purified—baptized by fire—and offer ourselves upon the golden altar.

On the altar:

1. We lose our attachment to our fleshly body. 2. We give up our material origin. 3. We recognize the flaws in all material means and methods. 4. We break our bondage to physical law.	Angels 1–4 Sound Rev. 8:2 –13
5. The Father's baptism unveils the mystery of evil as we discover that material losses cannot kill us, for God is our Life. 6. The Son's baptism demonstrates the Truth that overcomes the lie and takes us through the open door where we discover	Angels 5 & 6 Sound (Woes 1 & 2) Rev. 9
A LITTLE BOOK OPEN	Rev. 10
and	
A REED LIKE UNTO A ROD.	Rev. 11
7. We realize that perfect man is within our grasp and is inevitable, but we do not want to admit it. Must we really give birth to the grand idea so that "the mystery of God should be finished"? Yes!	Angel 7 Sounds (Woe 3) Rev. 11:14–19

A LITTLE BOOK OPEN

Rev. 10

Christ's purification method includes the blessings that enable us to see the final demonstration—baptism of the Holy Ghost. This little book, open in the angel's hand, was always available. However, for us it is a new discovery—something we could not see when vested in mortal mind.

The people who experienced the day of Pentecost may not have understood the full content of the little open book, but everyone there was struck with the realization of Truth that made them alive to God and to each other. God was present and death was dead. His disciples began to search the Torah for prophecies that had already been fulfilled and those that were being fulfilled before their eyes. They were amazed and thrilled when they found something that they had never noticed before. Those early students were learning that Christ presence and power pervade Scripture, awaiting only their comprehension and confirmation.

When Jesus was personally present on earth, he knew the contents of that book—understood God face to face—but he could not expound upon its contents because his disciples were not ready. He promised he would send a Comforter that would bring all things to their remembrance. In other words, the magnitude of his message would be *understood*—his message would become an *open book*.

As we follow Jesus' instructions and begin to understand how his works were accomplished, the OPEN BOOK will become written in our foreheads, and we will acknowledge our place as kings with Christ and the Father in His throne. It is God as *Love* that brings the promised Comforter to our conscious awareness.

Rev. 10

1 **And I saw another mighty angel come down from heaven, clothed with a cloud: and a rainbow was upon his head, and his face was as it were the sun, and his feet as pillars of fire:**

Audible revelation may be heard first as thunder, becoming a distinct voice from heaven only when one attains the proper ears to hear. As it is with ears, so it is with eyes. John's epiphany of Jesus' message is clothed with a cloud: at first he does not fully understand it. As his spiritual vision adjusts to the light, he is enabled to see all things clearly.

When we have eyes to read a message lit by God's light, we will also know the details of God's divine nature. Just as a rainbow divides light into its component colors, so will we understand the radiant contents of the message as well as the foundation on which it stands (his feet are aflame with Truth). The angel and little book stand intact in the flame, signifying their divine structure and refined purity.

2... **And he had in his hand a little book open:**

The size of this book does not denote its power. The modest Rosetta stone, enabling hieroglyphics to be deciphered, allowed ancient Egypt's language to be understood. In a vastly more important way, "a little book open" is a translator of Spirit. This symbolic title has not appeared before in Scripture, but the Ten Commandments and the Beatitudes are examples of Spirit language being translated into accessible form. The open book is the discovery that ultimately solves the mystery of God because it contains the key to being and the key to the bottomless pit (false being). Again, it is important to remember that we are not searching for form as a book, although a book may contain evidence of the key. We are searching for knowledge of God as a key. It is Mind's immediate knowledge, or *nous,* that is about to be discovered.

Of the ten virgins, five were wise with oil in their lamps. Their five exalted senses were "in the Spirit on the Lord's day" (Rev. 1:10). They were waiting and watching, expectant and prepared. When the Bridegroom came—when the door opened and the open book appeared—they went joyfully into the light to witness the wedding.

The mental composure of a wise virgin is the state of consciousness that is prepared to receive the gift of the second mighty angel. Jesus said, "I, if I be lifted up from the earth, will draw all men unto me" (John 12:32). The raising of Jesus above the earth to prepare for the reception of the Comforter means this: as we follow Jesus' methods, we begin to understand the power that lay behind them, and we recognize that *the way* he presented was not of the man Jesus but was the eternal Christ he manifested. As the physical appearance of Jesus ascended out of sight, the disciples' thoughts of him were lifted up to behold the *rock* underneath his word and works. When we acknowledge this rock, the way opens to the next enlightenment—a little book open.

…2 **and he set his right foot upon the sea, and his left foot on the earth,**

Earth or sea origins do not fool this mighty angel. Since the angel is literally God's thought, it never had any belief in a creator separate from God. Satan's mental suggestions and evolved material forms are put under the angel's feet. God's pure messengers stand impervious to erroneous influence.

3–4 **And cried with a loud voice, as when a lion roareth: and when he had cried, seven thunders uttered their voices. And when the seven thunders had uttered their voices, I was about to write: and I heard a voice from heaven saying unto me, Seal up those things which the seven thunders uttered, and write them not.**

The mighty angel holds within its grasp the enlightened message that will forever dissolve the darkness of ignorance. Evil thunders its objection, trying to mimic the might of Mind, but Christ's truth sword differentiates between good and evil—it will not allow us to trace error's path. In the presence of the open book, Satan's subterfuge of thunderous lies dies out unrecorded and unread.

5–6 **And the angel which I saw stand upon the sea and upon the earth lifted up his hand to heaven, And sware by him that liveth for ever and ever, who created heaven, and the things that therein are, and the earth, and the things that therein are, and the sea, and the things which are therein, that there should be time no longer:**

TIME NO LONGER identifies the magnitude and scale of this LITTLE OPEN BOOK and a REED LIKE A ROD. Their contents must be all-encompassing and final because prophecy ceases when they are read and understood. There will be nothing more to say and nothing to anticipate, for we will know the Truth and discover that we are made free, as Jesus promised in the Sermon on the Mount. The angel swears by God that heaven, earth, sea, and all their contents will experience this conscious phenomenon.

7 **But in the days of the voice of the seventh angel, when he shall begin to sound, the mystery of God should be finished, as he hath declared to his servants the prophets.**

Our true relationship with God is neither a mystery nor a miracle, and that union is soon to be understood.

> To him that overcometh will I grant to sit with me in my throne, even as I also overcame, and am set down with my Father in his throne (Rev. 3:21).

8–9 **And the voice which I heard from heaven spake unto me again, and said, Go and take the little book which is open in the hand of the angel which standeth upon the sea and upon the earth. And I went unto the angel, and said unto him, Give me the little book. And he said unto me, Take it, and eat it up; and it shall make thy belly bitter, but it shall be in thy mouth sweet as honey.**

As we have heard before in the opening of the seven seals, this grand illumination is not a free handout. Mortals need to strive for spiritual enlightenment. When we are able, we will reach out and take the little book, gratefully anticipating the predicted consequences.

10 **And I took the little book out of the angel's hand, and ate it up; and it was in my mouth sweet as honey: and as soon as I had eaten it, my belly was bitter.**

Tasting full knowledge of God is nothing less than a healing transformation, a sweet foretaste of home. Uncovering our own sin and disposing of it—giving up the things of this world in order to attain that transformation—is dauntingly difficult.

> I opened to my beloved; but my beloved had withdrawn himself, and was gone: my soul failed when he spake: I sought him, but I could not find him; I called him, but he gave me no answer (Song of Sol. 5:6).

11 **And he said unto me, Thou must prophesy again before many peoples, and nations, and tongues, and kings.**

We have just heard that prophecy would be finished with the sounding of the seventh trumpet, but the angel with the little book demands that John prophesy again. Revelation must be written in the minds of men before the seventh angel can be heard.

> Elias truly shall first come, and restore all things (Matt. 17:11).

Vision 3

A REED LIKE UNTO ROD

Rev. 11:1–13

1 And there was given me

A REED LIKE UNTO A ROD:

and the angel stood, saying,
Rise, and measure the temple of God, and
the altar, and
them that worship therein.

2 But the court which is without the temple leave out, and measure it not; for it is given unto the Gentiles: and the holy city shall they tread under foot forty and two months.

3 And I will give power unto my TWO WITNESSES, and they shall prophesy a thousand two hundred and threescore days, clothed in sackcloth.

4 These are the TWO OLIVE TREES, and the TWO CANDLESTICKS standing before the God of the earth.

5 And

if any man will hurt them, fire proceedeth out of their mouth, and devoureth their enemies: and

if any man will hurt them, he must in this manner be killed.

6 These

have power to shut heaven, that it rain not in the days of their prophecy:

and have power over waters to turn them to blood,

and to smite the earth with all plagues, as often as they will.

7 And when they shall have finished their testimony, the
beast that ascendeth out of the bottomless pit

shall make war against them, and
shall overcome them, and
kill them.

8 And their dead bodies shall lie in the street of the great city,
which spiritually is called Sodom and Egypt, where also
our Lord was crucified.

9 And they of the people and kindreds and tongues and
nations shall see their dead bodies three days and an half,
and shall not suffer their dead bodies to be put in graves.

10 And they that dwell upon the earth shall rejoice over them,
and make merry, and shall send gifts one to another;
because these two prophets tormented them that dwelt on
the earth.

11 And after three days and an half the Spirit of life from God
entered into them, and

they stood upon their feet;

and great fear fell upon them which saw them.

12 And they heard a great voice from heaven saying unto
them,

"Come up hither."

And **they ascended** up to heaven in a cloud; and their
enemies beheld them.

13 And the same hour was there a great earthquake, and the
tenth part of the city fell, and in the earthquake were slain
of men seven thousand: and

the remnant were affrighted,
and gave glory to the God of heaven.

Vision 3

A REED LIKE UNTO A ROD

Rev. 11:1–13

A LITTLE OPEN BOOK and a REED LIKE UNTO A ROD are the two final fulfillers of prophecy that enable us to realize our proper place and home while still on this plane of existence. Together they represent resurrection consciousness bringing in the Millennium, no longer touchable by the treasures or treacheries of this world but still visible in it. As we begin to understand how the OPEN BOOK manifests divine Mind as intelligent knowing, we will also see how a REED LIKE UNTO A ROD is the form of spiritual substance as body. The OPEN BOOK becomes written in our foreheads, giving us royal understanding as kings. A REED LIKE UNTO A ROD inscribes on our hearts the form and structure of Truth and Love as ministering priests.

> Thou art worthy to take the book, and to open the seals thereof: . . . And hast made us unto our God kings and priests: and we shall reign on the earth (Rev. 5:9–10).

1... **And there was given me a reed like unto a rod:**

A reed is a writing implement—a pen. A rod was used by shepherds to protect and guide sheep, and it was also a staff on which to lean. As Moses, Aaron, and their followers grew spiritually, the rod became a scepter of divine authority and power for guiding men. A rod is also a unit of measure.

> Oh that my words were now written! oh that they were printed in a book! That they were graven with an **iron pen** and lead in the rock for ever! (Job 19:23–24).

...1 **and the angel stood, saying, Rise, and measure the temple of God, and the altar, and them that worship therein.**

When Jesus declared, "Destroy this temple, and in three days I will raise it up" (John 2:19), he was referring to Christ consciousness rebuilding his physical body to correspond with his spiritual sense of body, which was untouchable by the crucifixion. Similarly, the angel is directing John—who now has an exalted understanding—to make an ironclad, written certification of the temple, the altar, and those who worship therein.

spiritual mind

The **Temple of God** is the forehead, or spiritual consciousness of the Word, that has the clarity of an open book. It is the *understanding* of Word that reigns with Christ on the throne.

spiritual sense

The Altar is the heart where the scepter pen engraves the might of divine Love. Priesthood presence humbly awaits every impression and reflects it back across Love's infinite universe.

spiritual activity

Them that worship therein is the experience of practicing the full realization of truth and love that makes life identical to the Truth and Love that created it.

When our thoughts coincide with the rectitude of this angel, a spiritual inclination will direct us to document our own spiritual sense of body.

2 **But the court which is without the temple leave out, and measure it not; for it is given unto the Gentiles: and the holy city shall they tread under foot forty and two months.**

Gentile thought is limited brain thinking that is still dominated by the senses. The testimony of the physical senses must be left out of the temple record, for one cannot measure the vastness of infinite Life and Love while contemplating the limited human condition. The Mind of God leaves brain waves outside, unconsidered and unworthy of comment.

Our sense of the infinite is somewhat limited by the appearance of a competitive physical sense. Forty-two months is 3½ years, which is half of 7. Until mortal mind is lost and forgotten, we are living in a halfway probationary period.

> No man hath ascended up to heaven, but he that came down from heaven, even the Son of man which is in heaven (John 3:13).

Every moment that we spend entertaining the physical senses or dreaming away the hours is denying Christ presence, treading the holy city under foot.

3 **And I will give power unto my two witnesses, and they shall prophesy a thousand two hundred and threescore days, clothed in sackcloth.**

The statement, "I am Alpha and Omega, the beginning and the ending" (Rev. 1:8), describes the premise for humanity's two witnesses. God's view is whole manifestation, whereas mankind witnesses a process of realization. To mankind, alpha is the dawning of Christ consciousness that spurs the mind to investigate something outside of itself. The product of that investigation is the first witness. Through many experiences of suffering, humility, repentance, and healing, one begins to understand something of the Mind of God until the full realization appears outside the limits of mortal consciousness. This is the omega, or last word, that brings the noontide experience of resurrection consciousness to man. The product of this realization is the second witness.

Christ comes to where we are, takes us by the hand, and lifts us up day by day to the realization of God with us. Divine Love never leaves heaven but draws us directly from above until we apprehend no separation between heaven and earth (until earth is heaven). Then we understand and embody Truth and Love.

Twelve hundred sixty days is again 3½ years, half of seven and time for repentance. As long as we have need of spiritual guides, they tarry with us.

4 **These are the two olive trees, and the two candlesticks standing before the God of the earth.**

Christ presents the *Truth*. All-embracing *Love* draws us to the Comforter that explains the Truth-Love relationship as an OPEN BOOK and a REED LIKE UNTO A ROD. Those individuals who manifest these qualities exemplify the two olive trees bearing the consecrated oil that heals and enlightens. They stand before God as two candlesticks, bearing the light for all to see: "Ye shall know them by their fruits" (Matt. 7:16).

Enlightened humanity identified Christ Jesus as the first witness because he exemplified an olive tree and a candlestick standing before God. Jesus prophesied that the one whom he would send in his name would be the Comforter, or Holy Ghost. The Woman clothed with the sun, introduced in chapter 12, typifies the figure that is enabled to receive the Comforter presence and decipher it for humanity.

5 **And if any man will hurt them, fire proceedeth out of their mouth, and devoureth their enemies: and if any man will hurt them, he must in this manner be killed.**

This is the divine method: the two-edged sword of truth, once seen, destroys the desire to sin. Because sin only exists in the mind of the sinner, it ceases to exist when the perfection of man is realized.

Jesus never spared the sternest condemnation of evil if it helped free a man from sin or hypocrisy. Such is the nature, place, and work of the first witness. Jesus met and mastered material sense, never succumbing to the temptations of this world. He demonstrated that heaven-sent Truth and heaven-abiding Love were available to him right here—he lived Truth and Love.

The second witness arrives when we stand at that holy place beside the ministering angel and receive the OPEN BOOK and REED LIKE UNTO A ROD from above. Then we will no longer be bound by the mystery of error, for the Comforter will have unveiled our foes. Love is the universal solvent and cannot know evil.

6–7 **These have power to shut heaven, that it rain not in the days of their prophecy: and have power over waters to turn them to blood, and to smite the earth with all plagues, as often as they will. And when they shall have finished their testimony, the beast that ascendeth out of the bottomless pit shall make war against them, and shall overcome them, and kill them.**

As John comprehends the spiritual substance underlying divine leadership, as expressed by the prophets, and witnesses the power of good to tread down all evil, he also sees the perilous persecution of anyone who actually proves the principle that breaks the chains of enslaved mortal man. The outward signs of the spiritual pioneers foretold the inward revolution that we all must experience when we drink of the same cup.

Once we recognize the truth of the OPEN BOOK and Love begins to reside in our hearts, we are forced to admit that no physical force can escape the control of omnipotent Spirit—no complex compound or mentally derived energy can outsmart Mind. The problem is that even as inspired humans, we are still partially living in the same mentality that is being outsmarted. We know we will have to die out of that mentality to break the boundaries of finite sense, but the evil mind that is still present in us concocts a scheme to preserve to the bitter end what is left of finite sense.

Because we are convinced of truth but have not yet proven it, the liar of all lies tempts us with one final challenge—*hypnotic complacency!* (See the seventh message to the church at Laodicea, Rev. 3:14–22). Self-satisfied that we have arrived at the open door and assuming that we already know the secret, we wander off into mind-numbing dreamland. Lulled by the serpent, we convince ourselves that we are saved, but we are really walking on the other side. Until we have evidence that we will survive the ordeal of the death of material sense, we fail to pass through the open door and, consequently, miss the opportunity to enter divine consciousness.

> And he cometh, and findeth them sleeping, and saith unto Peter, Simon, sleepest thou? couldest not thou watch one hour? (Mark 14:37).

Under the spell of hypnotic complacency, we unwittingly kill the two witnesses:

- We fail to wield the two-edged sword growing within our consciousness because to watch as Jesus watched demands us to cut off the right hand and pluck out the right eye (whatever is offensive). We become like the Pharisees of old who stupidly allowed Jesus to be killed rather than kill the evil within themselves.

- We kill the Comforter by either ignoring the advanced teaching that has been offered or by becoming satisfied with the intellectual exercise, thinking we are finished with The Revelation before we have turned to see the meaning from the Mind that is God.

8 **And their dead bodies shall lie in the street of the great city, which spiritually is called Sodom and Egypt, where also our Lord was crucified.**

For a time, we are stuck between two worlds, too drunk with astonishment at the great demands of truth to do anything to save ourselves. Christianity is not dead; it appears to be lifeless because it is not lived as Jesus lived it. By indulging in the traffic of superficial religion—and enslaving ourselves to the rich symbolism without understanding the spiritual significance—we crucify the Lord's purpose. When practical Christianity appears, the part of us that is still unenlightened sees a threat and moves to kill it. Spiritual enlightenment and the two witnesses are right in front of our faces, but they are dead to us—we have been found sleeping.

9 **And they of the people and kindreds and tongues and nations shall see their dead bodies three days and an half, and shall not suffer their dead bodies to be put in graves.**

Once we understand basic mathematics, we cannot go back to ignorance of its existence, even though we may resist using it. In the same way, once the BOOK is OPEN, as it is at this testing period, it can no longer be closed. We have become conscious of our own faults and instinctively know the Truth that has power over these faults. Spiritual wickedness discredits the messenger but cannot hide the vision of wisdom we have witnessed. We timidly poke at the edges of the solution but do not commit to do the work.

> Simon Peter saith unto them, I go a fishing. They say unto him, We also go with thee. They went forth, and entered into a ship immediately; and that night they caught nothing (John 21:3).

10 **And they that dwell upon the earth shall rejoice over them, and make merry, and shall send gifts one to another; because these two prophets tormented them that dwelt on the earth.**

In this hypnotic state of confusion, error screams louder than Love. Error appears to override our good moral intentions, even suggesting that if we preach the old way loud enough, we will not be able to hear spiritual consciousness at all. So we go on our merry way, choosing old time religion over spiritual enlightenment.

11 **And after three days and an half the Spirit of life from God entered into them, and they stood upon their feet; and great fear fell upon them which saw them.**

Light has no contest with darkness. Eventually, the Comforter is heard above the dull din of words without works.

At the morning meal after his resurrection, Jesus startled his prime students from their futile fishing expedition in the dark to the realization of practical abundance and a grand continuum of life. They were being prepared to take up their own crosses and fulfill their own missions. The seed of Christ must bear fruit of itself.

The devastating effects of our own mental drought stir our latent energies to prove what we know of truth and love. After a short trial, we resurrect our innate ability to behold the spirit of Life and reverently devote ourselves to the work.

12… **And they heard a great voice from heaven saying unto them, Come up hither.**

Figuratively, those who bring the concepts of Christ and the Comforter to humanity's notice are the martyrs who are killed, yet survive, and ascend up hither beyond any finite sense of life to the aliveness of infinite Being.

> These are the two anointed ones, that stand by the Lord of the whole earth (Zech. 4:14).

What is our reward for following in the Master's footsteps and receiving the OPEN BOOK and REED LIKE A ROD? When we have overcome sin, hypocrisy, death, and hell in ourselves, we too will hear the call to *come up hither!*

...12 **And they ascended up to heaven in a cloud; and their enemies beheld them.**

13 **And the same hour was there a great earthquake, and the tenth part of the city fell, and in the earthquake were slain of men seven thousand: and the remnant were affrighted, and gave glory to the God of heaven.**

Those who have ascended are no longer appreciable to those who have not because they are on different planes of existence; however, at the moment of ascension, the most advanced watchers are close enough to benefit from this spiritual transformation.

By Jesus' sublime example, his disciples were encouraged to shake themselves from the confines of their old convictions of life attached to earth. These faithful students were preparing for their own passage from sense to Soul. They had overcome ninety percent of their doubt, and the last ten percent fell away when they witnessed the ascension. The certainty of spiritual life was evident. They had found *the way.*

The OPEN BOOK and REED LIKE A ROD enable us to stand and witness the divine method of ascension for ourselves. These are all the tools necessary for us to take off our shoes, stand on holy ground, and wear the crown.

THE SEVENTH ANGEL SOUNDS

Rev. 11:14–19

14 The SECOND WOE is past; and, behold, the THIRD WOE
cometh quickly.

15 And the **seventh angel sounded**; and there were great
voices in heaven, saying, "The kingdoms of this world are
become the kingdoms of our Lord, and of his Christ; and he
shall reign for ever and ever."

16 And the four and twenty elders, which sat before God on
their seats, fell upon their faces, and worshipped God,
17 Saying,

*"We give thee thanks, O Lord God Almighty, which art,
and wast, and art to come; because thou hast taken to
thee thy great power, and hast reigned."*

18 And **the nations were angry**, and thy wrath is come, and
the time of the dead, that they should be judged, and that
thou shouldest give reward unto thy servants the prophets,
and to the saints, and them that fear thy name, small and
great; and shouldest destroy them which destroy the earth.

19 And the **temple of God was opened** in heaven, and there
was seen in his temple

THE ARK OF HIS TESTAMENT:

and there were lightnings, and voices, and thunderings, and an earthquake, and great hail.

Vision 3

The Seventh Angel Sounds

Rev. 11:14–19
Only five sentences are recorded after the seventh angel sounds. It is important not to be fooled by such brevity, for the prophetic conclusion is that ***"there should be time no longer"*** and ***"the mystery of God should be finished."*** Based on Jesus' headline announcements, these four verses predict the end of prophecy and the fulfillment of all prophecy. Is not this what we have been waiting for?

The sixth angel sounded the means for the realization of the seventh angel's message, assuring us that the solution to the problem of being is at hand.

14 **The second woe is past; and, behold, the third woe cometh quickly.**

This is the finale for Adam-and-Eve-based thinkers. It is the third wake up call: "My time is at hand."

15 **And the seventh angel sounded; and there were great voices in heaven, saying, The kingdoms of this world are become the kingdoms of our Lord, and of his Christ; and he shall reign for ever and ever.**

Ever since Adam saw himself cast out of Eden for disobeying God's command not to touch the knowledge of good and evil, man has felt himself separate from God. Mesmerized by its own self-interest, Adam's race has become unaware of its proximity to divinity. We learn in Scripture, however, that through much tribulation and patient obedience to Moses' Ten Commandments, we can rediscover our holy connection. As we put Jesus' Sermon on the Mount into practice, we find ourselves consecrated, ready to receive our dominion inheritance—to be now and forever at one with our Lord and his Christ.

16–17 **And the four and twenty elders, which sat before God on their seats, fell upon their faces, and worshipped God, Saying, We give thee thanks, O Lord God Almighty, which art, and wast, and art to come; because thou hast taken to thee thy great power, and hast reigned.**

The elders set the example and posture for receiving the Word. In wise humility, having no personal mind separate from God, they gratefully acknowledge the ever-presence of one omnipotent Mind.

18 **And the nations were angry, and thy wrath is come, and the time of the dead, that they should be judged, and that thou shouldest give reward unto thy servants the prophets, and to the saints, and them that fear thy name, small and great; and shouldest destroy them which destroy the earth.**

Revelation was written with mathematical precision. It unabashedly recorded the equations of God and man. The conclusions are absolute, and the relationship is always positive. So why is it that "the nations were angry"? Why did the nations reject the very gift from God that they had been seeking for millennia?

Try thinking a single thought forever. This sounds ridiculous to us since we cannot sustain a thought for more than a few seconds without repeating it. Therefore, it is just to conclude that our thoughts are both limited and finite. Christ questions us: 'What is the image and likeness of Truth? Can you picture it?' We answer, 'No!' Christ asks again, 'Can you measure omnipotence? Can you define omnipresence? Can you see Spirit? Can you describe infinite Love?' Again, we draw a blank. We cannot grasp unlimited concepts with a limited brain, so we turn away from the contemplation of them. The human mind cannot comprehend infinity. Therefore, it can neither grasp the fullness of God nor God's image and likeness, and that is why we cast Christ out.

Vision 3

> Now is the judgment of this world: now shall the prince of this world be cast out (John 12:31).

How will we survive this ordeal? God has power over our limitations, and Christ shepherds our conscience. The more we know of God, the less we are satisfied with this world. Do we like that? No! But it is inevitable. The prophets and saints have tasted heaven and are not dismayed by material losses; they push on to their reward.

Jesus prayed mightily that his cup might pass from him, but even his earthly body was temporarily killed. Nobody wants his or her finite concept of body to die. Even with the OPEN BOOK available and a REED ready to inscribe one's heart, we are reluctant to make the final necessary step and would rather hang on to a shred of finite form than to trust God with our lives as Spirit.

Jesus knew that his kingdom would be rejected (not understood) and would later be restored. Each stage of spiritual development requires a loss of some dearly held conviction and a gain of something more. We must even die out of millennial presence and awaken to infinite Mind, where we will behold a new heaven and a new earth. Then death and finiteness will no longer be chained in the bottomless pit. *Death* will be *forgotten*, lost in the infinity of Life.

One God has one image and likeness—one man (one man-I-festation). You may ask, 'Am I distinct?' We answer, 'Yes, but you are also infinite.'

19 **And the temple of God was opened in heaven, and there was seen in his temple the ark of his testament: and there were lightnings, and voices, and thunderings, and an earthquake, and great hail.**

We are the temple.

> Know ye not that ye are the temple of God, and that the Spirit of God dwelleth in you? If any man defile the temple of God, him shall God destroy; for the temple of God is holy, which temple ye are (1 Cor. 3:16–17).

And this is the promise fulfilled in your ears this day.

> I will put my law in their inward parts, and write it in their hearts; and will be their God, and they shall be my people (Jer. 31:33).

When Moses came down from the mount with the two tablets of stone from God, his face shone—he illustrated the effect of having the temple open for all to see. But the children of Israel insisted that he put a veil over his face. They were afraid to see the result of inspiration objectified.

The seventh angel proclaimed that the Ark of His Testament is within *us*. God-fed and God-aware consciousness is the principle of our very being. When the Temple of God is opened, the ark of His testament is the only evidence found. This fact is, indeed, sweet at its first taste, but we find its digestion bitter because we prefer *our way* to the First Commandment and *our choice* of sustenance to manna. Contemplating the inevitable fact that everything the prophets have said is true creates a tumult that shakes the human mind from its foundation until it gives up everything unlike God.

The pattern is now complete and the treasure, available. A LITTLE BOOK OPEN and a REED LIKE UNTO A ROD (the keys to the bottomless pit) are all the tools necessary for Life's realization. Perfect man is conceived, and we are ready to give birth to the grand idea.

Vision 4

A WOMAN CLOTHED WITH THE SUN & THE BIRTH OF THE MAN CHILD

Rev. 12

1 And there appeared a great wonder in heaven;

A WOMAN CLOTHED
WITH THE SUN,
and the
MOON UNDER HER FEET,
And upon her head a
CROWN OF TWELVE STARS:

2 And she being with child cried,
travailing in birth, and pained to be
delivered.

3 And there appeared another wonder in
heaven; and behold a

GREAT RED DRAGON,
having
SEVEN HEADS
and
TEN HORNS,
and
SEVEN CROWNS
upon his heads.

4 And his tail drew the third part of the stars
of heaven, and did cast them to the earth:
and the dragon stood before the woman
which was ready to be delivered, for to
devour her child as soon as it was born.

5 **And she brought forth A MAN CHILD, who was to rule all nations with a rod of iron: and her child was caught up unto God, and to his throne.**

6 And the woman fled into the wilderness, where she hath a place prepared of God, that they should feed her there a thousand two hundred and threescore days.

7 AND THERE WAS WAR IN HAVEN:
Michael and his angels fought
against the dragon;

and the dragon fought and his angels,
8 **and prevailed not; neither was their place**
found any more in heaven.

9 And **the great dragon was cast out**, that old serpent, called the Devil, and Satan, which deceiveth the whole world: he was cast out into the earth, and his angels were cast out with him.

10 And I heard a loud voice saying in heaven, "Now is come salvation, and strength, and the kingdom of our God, and the power of his Christ: for **the accuser of our brethren is cast down**, which accused them before our God day and night.

11 And **they overcame him by the blood of the Lamb, and by the word of their testimony; and they loved not their lives unto the death.**

12 Therefore rejoice, ye heavens, and ye that dwell in them. **Woe to the inhabiters of the earth and of the sea! for the devil is come down unto you**, having great wrath, because he knoweth that he hath but a short time."

13 And when the dragon saw that he was cast unto the earth, he persecuted the woman which brought forth the man child.

14 And to the woman were given two
wings of a great eagle, that she might
fly into the wilderness, into her
place, where she is nourished for a
time, and times, and half a time,
from the face of the serpent.

15 And the serpent cast out of his mouth water
as a flood after the woman, that he might
cause her to be carried away of the flood.

16 **And the earth helped the woman, and the earth opened
her mouth, and swallowed up the flood which the
dragon cast out of his mouth.**

17 And the dragon was wroth with the woman,
and went to make war with the remnant of
her seed, which keep the commandments of
God, and have the testimony of Jesus Christ.

A Woman Clothed with the Sun & the Birth of the Man Child

Scientific Obstetrics

Rev. 12

Jesus' Revelation has prepared us and led us to this moment. Now "ye must be born again" (John 3:7). In allegorical terms, we are about to witness God's method of universal salvation and the destruction of all sin, hypocrisy, death, and hell. The LITTLE BOOK OPEN has been digested, and a REED LIKE A ROD has transformed the human heart. Now it is time for Jesus' most obscure prophesies to be realized—his promises fulfilled.

1 **And there appeared a great wonder in heaven; a woman clothed with the sun, and the moon under her feet, and upon her head a crown of twelve stars:**

The Woman symbolizes the highest form of Love's (God's) manifestation—Motherhood. This prototype figure is not clothed in a cloud, or cloaked in mystery; she is a life-bright witness, ready to bring forth her conception of the man child—God's man in perfect harmony (heaven). This is what a lit candlestick looks like. She stands for both Principle and practice. Her thoughts radiate outward and upward, above material conditions and consequences. In the dark night of chaos, we are grateful for moonlight reflected from the sun, but when the Comforter dawns upon human consciousness, the dim distortions are put under foot. Twelve stars encircle her mental heaven.

Throughout Scripture, as voiced by every prophet, God has promised us an inheritance. Could this inheritance be figured as twelve stars? If so, each star represents a redeemed birthright.

Our inheritance was identified in the letters to the churches.

To him that overcometh will 'I' give:

1. the tree of life;
2. a crown of life;
3. the hidden manna;
4. a white stone, and in the stone a new name written;
5. power over the nations;
6. the morning star;
7. white raiment;
8. his name not blotted out of the book of life but confessed before my Father and before his angels;
9. a pillar in the temple of my God;
10. the name of my God and the name of the city of my God, which is New Jerusalem written upon him;
11. my new name written upon him;

12. And "to him that overcometh will I grant to sit with me in my throne, even as I also overcame, and am set down with my Father in his throne."

To wear the crown is to have dominion over all the woes suffered by the twelve tribes of Israel and over all men in their pursuit of the Promised Land, which now is understood to be a wholly spiritual state of dominion consciousness.

Moses heard God's mothering directive long ago in the wilderness: "Carry them in thy bosom, as a nursing father beareth the sucking child" (Num. 11:12).

Now the true Promised Land is about to be occupied.

2 **And she being with child cried, travailing in birth, and pained to be delivered.**

This grand type of noble womanhood is "to be delivered." There is no question of her success, no pain from anxiety, and no fear of failure. "Travailing in birth" is the mental energy expended to see the window of heaven open. Her virgin consecration enabled her to conceive the idea of perfect man, and the Comforter is about to deliver her sweet promise.

3 **And there appeared another wonder in heaven; and behold a great red dragon, having seven heads and ten horns, and seven crowns upon his heads.**

Just as the serpent showed up without invitation in the Garden of Eden, so it flaunts its image again in a more demanding way. It appears larger now because we know from bitter experience more about evil than we did in the beginning. Its subtle suggestions, once thought to be incidental, now pervade the entire landscape of finite thought. We concur with Solomon: there is "no profit under the Sun" (Eccl. 2:11).

Right at the moment of our highest demonstration of spiritual birth, we are tempted to heed a thought that God did not think. Evil masterfully parades with all the paraphernalia of a king in heaven, but it is a charade designed to mock God. There are several clues to the dragon's falsehood. Its red color tantalizes the eyes, but it is an incomplete idea as only one band in the color spectrum. Seven heads cannot contain one Mind, although the number seven mimics completeness. (Biblically, the number seven can represent all good or all evil.) Ten horns would deny the Commandments by claiming that it is possible to bear one's own body—be self-made—contrary to Truth. Anything that would oppose our translation back to spiritual consciousness is the dragon. This so-called wonder in heaven is a momentary reenactment of every evil thought since Adam.

4 **And his tail drew the third part of the stars of heaven, and did cast them to the earth: and the dragon stood before the woman which was ready to be delivered, for to devour her child as soon as it was born.**

Believe what the head is saying, and you must suffer the consequences of the dragon's tail. Sin and hypocrisy produce a tail of guilt and separation. (Adam and Eve felt naked and alone after indulging in a lie.)

The dragon cleverly attempts to mimic the effect of the fourth cleansing angel when a third part of the stars were darkened (Rev. 8:12). The fourth angel's purpose was to alert us to the fallacy of believing in a matter-based universe. The dragon's purpose is the mirror opposite: to dissuade us from reuniting with our spiritual universe. Evil attacks our progress at every advancing stage, but just look at its lack of accomplishment: it failed to keep Jesus buried in the tomb, it failed to keep the book sealed, it was burned up on the altar, and it failed to hold the Woman forever ignorant of God. Now the Woman is pregnant with the idea of understanding spiritual man, just as Jesus' mother, Mary, prefigured it. Since evil cannot overthrow the Woman's concept, it threatens to attack the product, like Herod did as soon as Jesus was born. Evil threatens but cannot kill the birth of a spiritual idea because it has no such capability.

5 **And she brought forth a man child, who was to rule all nations with a rod of iron: and her child was caught up unto God, and to his throne.**

Only ideas that are conceived in heaven can be caught up unto heaven, and those spiritual forms must include all the qualities of Father-Mother God—omnipotent, omniscient, omnipresent, and omni-acting Life, Truth, Love. This holy birth is not formed in a womb; it is a mental realization, a compound idea of man born of Mind. In addition, for God to be called *creator*, God must be forever creating and must be the originator of every conception. Therefore, it must be true that the man child caught up unto God is not a singular event; it is a continuous event, distinctly realized.

Who is this enlightened one clothed with the sun; who is the man child caught up unto heaven? It is *you as you really are,* pregnant with the nous of perfect man; it is everyone realizing God's one whole creation, born mature in exquisite harmony; it is Woman bringing the real man of God's creating into view; it is Motherhood bringing forth Manhood; it is the Lamb wearing the crown of glory; it is love knowing the Truth.

When this message is born to inspired humanity, we are sure that God is with us governing Mind's every thought "with a rod of iron." We are no longer earthbound but born again as "one like unto the Son of man," sitting with the Lamb on the throne.

6 **And the woman fled into the wilderness, where she hath a place prepared of God, that they should feed her there a thousand two hundred and threescore days.**

Again, 1260 days is 3½ years (half of 7) and signifies a *transitional* place or time. Joseph saved his brothers and all of Egypt from starvation. Moses guided the children of Israel into the desert, where they were safe from external domination. These progenitors of the Woman prophesied the time when the early symbols would be relived from within, where "the still small voice" of truth would mature into the guiding star of being.

7–8 **And there was war in heaven: Michael and his angels fought against the dragon; and the dragon fought and his angels, And prevailed not; neither was their place found any more in heaven.**

The term *heaven* in this context means the human mental experience in which both God's message and Satan's message can be heard. This is war within! Proper warfare of this type can only take place after the OPEN BOOK and a REED LIKE A ROD begin to become apparent.

In this world, we are offered endless opportunities to think our own thoughts, fight our own battles, and indulge in our own pleasures. Only after we gain the awareness of the Comforter do we begin to lose our desire and power to act independently. When we bow before Christ, Truth, and patiently wait on God—when we lay down our suffering and lay bare our sin, ready to see what God thinks—Michael and his angels fight our battles for us. Darkness cannot prevail over the light of Christ.

9 **And the great dragon was cast out, that old serpent, called the Devil, and Satan, which deceiveth the whole world: he was cast out into the earth, and his angels were cast out with him.**

Casting the dragon out is no small feat, for it involves removing the entire mass of error within oneself. This is neither about overcoming our childhood fears and fantasies nor about overcoming our untimely birth. We must overcome our *conception* as mortals. We must ultimately understand that we are "without father, without mother, without descent, having neither beginning of days, nor end of life; but made like unto the Son of God" (Heb. 7:3). Evil will have no place when this understanding comes, for it is cast into the earth—ground to dust and nothingness—along with all the suggestions (angels) that proposed material conception in the first place. We must come to the conclusion that matter and energy have no intelligence.

10 **And I heard a loud voice saying in heaven, Now is come salvation, and strength, and the kingdom of our God, and the power of his Christ: for the accuser of our brethren is cast down, which accused them before our God day and night.**

Finally, we can hear the voice declaring our freedom and strength; we can feel Love's omnipresence and trust Truth's omnipotence because the massive confusion—conception formed in matter—is cast out. The accuser who ruled the day and night (good and evil) of all human misconceptions is cast down. Now, in the clear shining of noonday has come salvation, and the prophecy "that there should be time no longer" is fulfilled. God and His thoughts (Mind and manifestation) is all there is to the universe, for we are brethren of one stupendous whole.

11 **And they overcame him by the blood of the Lamb, and by the word of their testimony; and they loved not their lives unto the death.**

They overcame the accuser by living divine Love and by the word of truth that Christ delivered; they loved not the things of this world, not even their own bodily sense of life, until the evil of it died away.

When we love as Jesus loved, understand the truths he taught, and live the mind of Christ as he did, we must conclude that Satan has no life to offer and, therefore, cannot take it away. When we do this, we will have mastered the belief in a life apart from God.

Life does not begin when we die. We recognize Life when we give up our mortal sense of it. Life lived does not require us to die physically. It requires that we escape the slavery of the senses—sin, hypocrisy, death, and hell. What we think of as life's journey is finished when we break the stricture of belief in death. Then time disappears, and all prophecy is fulfilled, for we are made as new and live in the *now*.

We have no life of our own. God is Life living us. We cannot love of ourselves. God is Love loving us into existence. Understanding the truth about Life and Love transforms human consciousness in a way that demonstrates our comprehension of man as sons and daughters of God. Death by transformation of consciousness leads to *life lived*.

12 **Therefore rejoice, ye heavens, and ye that dwell in them. Woe to the inhabiters of the earth and of the sea! for the devil is come down unto you, having great wrath, because he knoweth that he hath but a short time.**

Dwelling in the consciousness of *life lived*, we are completely separate from the cares and temptations of this world. This was Jesus' normal mental state, and biblical testimony declares that John attained it as well, proving that it is possible to be heaven conscious and still be visible to the world. However, there is no hope of attaining this consciousness without a thorough cleansing.

Human experience is full of woe until we concede to the two witnesses. How long it takes before we give up *our way* and be with Christ on the throne depends upon the tenacity of evil. In Spirit language, time is infinite *now*. Time that is finite, time that can be measured, is a short time. Be assured that Christ will never leave us as we acquire this Life awareness. Jesus said, "I am with you alway, even unto the end of the world" (Matt. 28:20).

13 **And when the dragon saw that he was cast unto the earth, he persecuted the woman which brought forth the man child.**

It is interesting to note that the dragon has no power to choose its domain. (The only power it ever has is the undeserved credit we give it.) The same malicious instinct that failed to eradicate the word and works of the Master now attacks the Woman. Salvation from all evil influence is certain, but not until we recognize and give gratitude for the Woman and her work. She exemplifies Love enacting love.

14 **And to the woman were given two wings of a great eagle, that she might fly into the wilderness, into her place, where she is nourished for a time, and times, and half a time, from the face of the serpent.**

Demonstrable expressions of Womanhood must be tested and proven in the wilderness without using the world's means, for virtue flies above earth's limitations. Spiritual pinions alone prove and sustain grace, hiding her from the serpent's face. Christ says, "Get thee behind me, Satan" (Matt. 16:23). Correspondingly, the serpent is behind the Woman because she has turned away from it as her claimed identity. Facing good, we inevitably move toward it and away from sin and hypocrisy. The probationary period is, again, 3 ½ — time (1) and times (2) and half a time (½).

15 **And the serpent cast out of his mouth water as a flood after the woman, that he might cause her to be carried away of the flood.**

After the demonstration of God's Motherhood and the witnessing of the man child caught up unto God, evil floods the brain with amazement, screaming, 'You cannot do that!' Old theology will do anything to halt progress in order to preserve its traditions. Did men not conspire to kill Jesus for this very reason? Keeping the veil in place preserves the peace for earth-based thinkers and keeps them dead to Christ.

16 **And the earth helped the woman, and the earth opened her mouth, and swallowed up the flood which the dragon cast out of his mouth.**

When we know God, we trust both the message and the messenger. With the Word of God in his mouth, Moses could say with confidence, "Hereby ye shall know that the Lord hath sent me to do all these works; for I have not done them of mine own mind" (Num 16:28). Now it is the Woman who wears the crown of God's Mind.

The works of honest laborers—genuine healing in the Christ field—swallow up the flood that would discredit Womanhood's accomplishments. These good people hear their Master's voice repeating itself. They know the truth about Love and rally behind the Woman within themselves, for she represents the final proof of the man child's true identity.

> And it shall come to pass in the last days, saith God, I will pour out of my Spirit upon all flesh: and your sons and your daughters shall prophesy, and your young men shall see visions, and your old men shall dream dreams:
> (Acts 2:17).

17 **And the dragon was wroth with the woman, and went to make war with the remnant of her seed, which keep the commandments of God, and have the testimony of Jesus Christ.**

The dragon has failed again and again to halt the path of progress, and it will continue to fail until it is no longer tolerated. The man child caught up unto God is beyond the dragon's reach, and the Woman will not listen nor be impressed; only the Woman's legacy, the remnant of her seed, is subject to attack. Her resources (a LITTLE BOOK OPEN and a REED LIKE A ROD), her works, and all those who would attempt to learn from her example are under attack. If these resources were to be lost, the Comforter promised by Jesus would be hidden from humanity.

Disparaging remarks, incorrect publishing, misinformation, discouragement, quarrelling among disciples, monotonous sermons, words without works, lies, laziness, alternatives to Christ, hypocrisy, ineffective prayers, belief without understanding, secrecy, and doctrines of men flood the minds of would-be-enlightened humanity in an attempt to preserve the ultimate enemy—ignorance of oneself. However, we know that the dragon has no power to alter prophecy or its fulfillment, since disorientation and confusion has "but a short time." Eventually, the flood of misinformation will be seen as a subterfuge.

> Verily I say unto you, This generation shall not pass away, till all be fulfilled. Heaven and earth shall pass away: but my words shall not pass away (Luke 21:32–33).

The Womanhood of God and Her resources have been discovered, illustrated, and proven. When the legacy of the Woman is repeated in the minds of men, sin and hypocrisy will be null and void, death and hell will be obsolete, and there will be finite "time no longer."

This chapter concludes the record of the divine method of redemption. The one caught up unto God and his throne and the Woman clothed with the sun have realized the new heaven and new earth.

Chapters 13 through 18 illustrate a magnified reenactment of the dragon's warfare with the remnant through the distorted lens of human eyes and stubborn human will. This warfare appears to cause terrible suffering and loss, but it also instigates resurrection consciousness (chapters 19 and 20) and the ascension (chapters 21–22:2).

> These things I have spoken unto you, that in me ye might have peace. In the world ye shall have tribulation: but be of good cheer; I have overcome the world (John 16:33).

Vision 4

THE DRAGON'S TWO FALSE WITNESSES

View from the Sand of the Sea

Rev. 13

1 And I stood upon the **SAND OF THE SEA**, and saw

A BEAST
rise up out of the sea, having
SEVEN HEADS
And
TEN HORNS,
and upon his horns
TEN CROWNS,
and upon his heads the name of
BLASPHEMY.

2 And the beast which I saw was **like unto a leopard**, and
his feet were as the **feet of a bear**, and his mouth as **the**
mouth of a lion: and the dragon gave him his power, and
his seat, and great authority.

3 And I saw one of his heads as it were wounded to death;
and **his deadly wound was healed**: and all the world
wondered after the beast.
4 And **they worshipped the dragon** which gave power unto
the beast: and **they worshipped the beast**, saying,

"Who is like unto the beast?
who is able to make war with him?"

5 And there was given unto him a mouth speaking great
things and blasphemies; and power was given unto him to
continue forty and two months.
6 And he opened his mouth in blasphemy against God, to
blaspheme
his name, and
his tabernacle, and
them that dwell in heaven.

7 And it was given unto him to make war with the saints, and to overcome them: and power was given him over all kindreds, and tongues, and nations.

8 And all that dwell upon the earth shall worship him, whose names are not written in the book of life of the Lamb slain from the foundation of the world.

9 **If any man have an ear, let him hear.**

10 **He that leadeth into captivity shall go into captivity: he that killeth with the sword must be killed with the sword.**

Here is the patience and the faith of the saints.

11 And I beheld

ANOTHER BEAST
coming up out of the earth; and he had
TWO HORNS
like a lamb, and he spake as a
DRAGON.

12 And he exerciseth all the power of the first beast before him, and causeth the earth and them which dwell therein to **worship the first beast,** whose deadly wound was healed.

13 And he doeth great wonders, so that he maketh

FIRE COME DOWN FROM HEAVEN
on the earth in the sight of men,

14 And **deceiveth them that dwell on the earth by the**
means of those miracles which he had power to do in the
sight of the beast; saying to them that dwell on the earth,
that
they should make an image to the beast,
which had the wound by a sword, and did live.

15 And he had power to give life unto the image of the beast,
that the image of the beast should both speak, and cause
that as many as would not worship the image of the beast
should be killed.
16 And he causeth all, both small and great, rich and poor, free
and bond, to receive
a mark in their right hand, or in their foreheads:

17 And that no man might buy or sell, save he that had the
mark, or the name of the beast, or the number of his name.

18 Here is wisdom. Let him that hath understanding count the
number of the beast: for it is the number of

A MAN;

and his number is

SIX HUNDRED THREESCORE AND SIX.

The Dragon's Two False Witnesses

VIEW FROM THE SAND OF THE SEA

The Dragon's Business

Rev. 13

Michael and his angels correctly classified the dragon as "cast unto the earth." Jesus had said this about Satan before, at a time when the seventy had returned from casting out devils: "I beheld Satan as lightning fall from heaven" (Luke 10:18). Therefore, it is fair to say that the dragon is not part of God's universe. But God is all, so the dragon must stand for the suppositional opposite—a false, misdirected sense of good evolved from nothing. Jesus' angel illustrates the nature and character of the dragon by two beasts, or false witnesses, who are deceived into believing that they have amazing powers and an amazing god. This chapter reveals the method the dragon uses to make war with us.

1 **And I stood upon the sand of the sea, and saw a beast rise up out of the sea, having seven heads and ten horns, and upon his horns ten crowns, and upon his heads the name of blasphemy.**

Sand represents the supposition that evil has the power to grind the rock, Christ, into powder and mold it into its own image. John was enabled to stand and view the dragon's intent and operation without being personally influenced. Behold the view from the shifting sands of the dragon's mind!

John saw the dragon conceive something that looked like a man, but it was evolved from animated atoms into slime and then into a beast of flesh and blood. This pseudo man could trace the dragon's messages with an electron brain and be fooled into thinking that it was thinking. It believed it could think anything. Animated by the dragon like a puppet, it thought it had power to deny the seven spirits of God, mock the Ten Commandments, and wear crowns of self-indulgence. This seemed all well and good to the beast man, but in reality he was almost totally self-ignorant. The dragon's sole purpose is to keep the flesh man ignorant so that he will never seek the truth.

2 **And the beast which I saw was like unto a leopard, and his feet were as the feet of a bear, and his mouth as the mouth of a lion: and the dragon gave him his power, and his seat, and great authority.**

According to the dragon, the beast is to be governed by animal instincts within the survival-of-the-fittest paradigm. The beast is designed to expand by consuming others. Although he thinks himself to be an intellectual treasure, he is more likely to use brute force than reason. To catch his unsuspecting prey, he lurks in the dark, mirroring the dragon's inclinations, ignorant of the possibility of enlightenment. When out from under cover, the beast is loudmouthed, self-willed, and boastful, which is a sure sign of lack of content.

> All these things will I give thee, if thou wilt fall down and worship me (Matt. 4:9).

3 **And I saw one of his heads as it were wounded to death; and his deadly wound was healed: and all the world wondered after the beast.**

Functionally, this fleshly creature is absolutely amazing! If it gets wounded, its body immediately goes to work to heal itself. It just gets better without asking anything of the beast. To entice its victim to submit to its system, the dragon provides a display of inexplicable wonder.

4 **And they worshipped the dragon which gave power unto the beast: and they worshipped the beast, saying, Who is like unto the beast? who is able to make war with him?**

Self-healing wounds are impressive to the beast man, who is prone to accidents and failure. As a result, he religiously subscribes to the health laws laid out by the dragon—mortal mind—in order to encourage a repetition of the wonder. He also worships the body for having its own healing capability. When one is hurting, who can argue with relief?

5 **And there was given unto him a mouth speaking great things and blasphemies; and power was given unto him to continue forty and two months.**

The serpent in Genesis 3:3–4 was the first to contradict God. Speaking of the tree of good and evil, "God hath said, Ye shall not eat of it, neither shall ye touch it, lest ye die. And the serpent said unto the woman, *Ye shall not surely die.*" This boast of the serpent that purports to know more than God is our guide to damnation all the years of our trials on earth.

6 **And he opened his mouth in blasphemy against God, to blaspheme his name, and his tabernacle, and them that dwell in heaven.**

Once the fruit of good and evil is tasted, and the brain begins to believe what it sees and to desire more of it, every moment of mortal consciousness is blasphemy against the seven spirits of God, against the harmony of only good, and against all those who never tasted of the tree of clever defiance.

7 **And it was given unto him to make war with the saints, and to overcome them: and power was given him over all kindreds, and tongues, and nations.**

The physical senses can neither understand the consciousness of divine Love nor understand those who have attained spiritual consciousness. Ignorance that defies the path to wisdom may martyr the wise in order to justify its stupid stance, thereby denying others access to the true witnesses, who are so helpful to those seeking enlightenment. All manner of peoples and tongues and nations may embrace ignorance as a way to defy God, all the while claiming "thy will be done" (Matt. 6:10).

8 **And all that dwell upon the earth shall worship him, whose names are not written in the book of life of the Lamb slain from the foundation of the world.**

We secretly and openly acknowledge that we are naughty and think it is fun, but the fact remains that while we are entertaining devils, we are unconscious of good. Not one microbe of evil is written in the Lamb's book of life. As long as we claim the beast as us, we will never know our real identity.

As viewed from the sand of the sea, the dragon has slain the Lamb and will continue to slay it as long as sin remains a functional reality. The effort of evil to destroy divine Love's representative proves that worldliness is the foundation of the dragon's lair.

9 **If any man have an ear, let him hear.**

Christ conscience is describing our faults and susceptibilities. Are we seeking correction?

10 **He that leadeth into captivity shall go into captivity: he that killeth with the sword must be killed with the sword. Here is the patience and the faith of the saints.**

Individually, whatever we think or do that God did not enact is subscribing to a law defined by the dragon. If we accept sin and death to be law, then we experience those conditions. Christ knows nothing of pain and suffering, yet these devices often propagate the very repentance and correction needed to bring us to Christ.

A law governing a city knows nothing of the people affected by that law and nothing of the consequences to the individuals who disobey that law; nevertheless, the purpose of the punishment for disobedience is to bring about compliance to the law. This is the divine method of correction. To have saintly presence in the city of our God is to comply with God's law—the law of good.

11 **And I beheld another beast coming up out of the earth; and he had two horns like a lamb, and he spake as a dragon.**

On a more complex plane than the pseudo man is a more potent force that acts by hidden mental methods to control physical phenomena. When the human mind begins to develop this capability, it thinks it has found the Holy Grail, but in reality, it is the dragon defining itself. Posing as the high priest of God, it wears a body with two horns and a manipulative mental mind. Confidently broadcasting its sovereignty, Satan exclaims, "God doth know that in the day ye eat thereof, then your eyes shall be opened, and ye shall be as gods, knowing good and evil" (Gen 3:5).

12 **And he exerciseth all the power of the first beast before him, and causeth the earth and them which dwell therein to worship the first beast, whose deadly wound was healed.**

We worship matter because we are ignorant of the Truth, hate Truth, and prefer a healthy body (which we can see) to Spirit. It is much easier to worship Jesus' body, which was raised from the dead, than it is to follow his demands faithfully.

13–14 **And he doeth great wonders, so that he maketh fire come down from heaven on the earth in the sight of men, And deceiveth them that dwell on the earth by the means of those miracles which he had power to do in the sight of the beast; saying to them that dwell on the**

earth, that they should make an image to the beast, which had the wound by a sword, and did live.

Like the ancient necromancers in Egypt, but now much more complicated and subtle, the dragon worshipper of today kneels in pseudo prayer and produces convincing evidence of the power of the mind to mimic God's wonders and affect a person's health. Once we become convinced of the mental nature of the universe, knowing that what we see is a mental manifestation of our own thought, we believe we are free to experiment.

The most deceptive thing the dragon has ever done is to show how to heal the sick by mental brainpower. Then it attaches a picture of Jesus' crucifixion to the process and calls it faith healing. This false type of faith healing is impressive and cannot be explained by physics, so the dragon calls it a form of religion. To the deceived mind, Jesus' pierced body has become the object upon which to attach all blessings and blame, no matter what method of false religion produces the belief. Ignorantly, we have been fooled once again to worship an idol rather than Christ. Such is the nature of mortal mind.

15 **And he had power to give life unto the image of the beast, that the image of the beast should both speak, and cause that as many as would not worship the image of the beast should be killed.**

We empower idols by the faith we attach to them, but it is the evil mind behind the faith that animates physical forms. Dragon worship is another name for mortal mind, which makes matter appear to live in the form of a mortal body. Amazed by a sense of self-conscious awareness, this man made of flesh will send to its death anything unlike himself, even the saints of God. Mortal man can never understand God or God's image and likeness.

16–17 **And he causeth all, both small and great, rich and poor, free and bond, to receive a mark in their right hand, or in their foreheads: And that no man might buy or sell, save he that had the mark, or the name of the beast, or the number of his name.**

The beast is self-conscious matter in all its forms, and the image of the beast is the elementary evil that empowers the beast. The material body cannot think, but the image of the beast (mortal mind) builds a brain that justifies itself, buys into its own dream, and believes nothing but its own evidence. Until we are born again—God conscious—we identify with the image of the beast, love the beast, and spread the beast's story.

18 **Here is wisdom. Let him that hath understanding count the number of the beast: for it is the number of a man; and his number is Six hundred threescore and six.**

At the time Saint John's Revelation was copied onto papyrus, the decimal point had not yet been invented. However, placing a decimal point before 666 gives us .666, which equals the fraction two-thirds. There are several places where the dragon attempts to destroy a third of something. John uses one-third and two-thirds as symbols to identify the dragon's work and to designate where Truth is nullifying the effect of the dragon.

Also, notice that it is *'a'* man who is identified. *'A'* can refer to an individual or type of man—one of many. God has infinite ideas, but if we were to designate them correctly, they all would be the number *one* because they are the image and likeness of One. To differentiate the beast man's identity from the man of God's creating, Jesus' messenger gives him the number six.

We know that the number seven stands for wholeness. *Six* is an attempt that appears to come close to the mark but misses it. The number 666 stands for finiteness, division, and lack of completeness. Three times in Scripture and in three ways evil tries to destroy us, and each time it fails.

-6- First, we are enticed with pleasurable suggestions to be a little mischievous, just as **Eve was tempted in the Garden of Eden:** to have desires other than God, to have choices to obey or not, to have *what if* mentalities, to have self-will, to live separately unto ourselves, to have pleasures of self-aggrandizement, to feel a little lustful, to be sneaky, to cheat a little and get away with it, to think we can do it all by ourselves, and to temporarily tune out our shepherd leader.

-6- Second, evil attempts to enforce slavery by inflicting itself upon humanity: **The dragon made war with the remnant of her seed.** This illustrates evil's obduracy. Satan's threats appear as our own thoughts: 'Use my money, or you will starve.' 'Obey physical law, or I will make you sick.' 'Obey the medical arts, or I will keep you sick.' 'Fill your life with busyness—friends, music, chores, culture, children, money, work—or you will feel lonely and empty.' With dire consequences, evil attempts to force us to continue on the path back to dust, even claiming that God will punish us if we do not submit to human beliefs and faith without works.

-6- Third, death attempts to stagnate man's progress toward the ascension when **Satan is let loose after being bound during the Millennium.** (This topic is covered later in chapter 20.)

VIEW FROM MOUNT SION

Rev. 14

1 And I looked, and, lo,

a Lamb stood on THE MOUNT SION,

and with him an hundred forty and four thousand, having
his Father's name written in their foreheads.

2 And I heard a voice from heaven, as the voice of many
waters, and as the voice of a great thunder: and I heard the
voice of harpers harping with their harps:
3 And they
sung as it were A NEW SONG before the throne
and before the four beasts, and the elders:

and no man could learn that song but the hundred and forty and four thousand, which were redeemed from the earth.

4
- These are they which were not defiled with women; for they **are virgins**.
- These are they which **follow the Lamb** whithersoever he goeth.
- These were **redeemed from among men**, being the firstfruits unto God and to the Lamb.

5
- And in their mouth was found **no guile**: for they are **without fault** before the throne of God.

6 And I saw another angel fly in the midst of heaven, having
the everlasting gospel to preach unto them that dwell on the
earth, and to every nation, and kindred, and tongue, and
people,
7 Saying with a loud voice,

"**Fear God**, and **give glory** to him; for the hour of his judgment is come: and **worship** him that made heaven, and earth, and the sea, and the fountains of waters."

8 And there followed another angel, saying,

"**Babylon is fallen, is fallen**, that great city, because she
made all nations drink of the wine of the wrath of her
fornication."

9 And the third angel followed them, saying with a loud
voice,

**"If any man worship the beast and his image, and
receive his mark in his forehead, or in his hand,**
10 **The same shall drink of the wine of the wrath of God,
which is poured out without mixture into the cup of his
indignation; and he shall be tormented with fire and
brimstone in the presence of the holy angels, and in the
presence of the Lamb":**

11 And the smoke of their torment ascendeth up for ever and
ever: and **they have no rest day nor night, who worship
the beast and his image**, and whosoever receiveth the
mark of his name.

12 Here is **the patience of the saints:**
here are they that keep the commandments of God, and the
faith of Jesus.

13 And I heard a voice from heaven saying unto me,
"Write, **Blessed are the dead which die in the Lord** from
henceforth":
"Yea," saith the Spirit,
**"that they may rest from their labours;
and their works do follow them."**

14 And I looked, and behold a white cloud, and upon the cloud
one sat LIKE UNTO THE SON OF MAN,
having on his head a
GOLDEN CROWN,
and in his hand a
SHARP SICKLE.

15 And another angel came out of the temple, crying with a
loud voice to him that sat on the cloud,

"Thrust in thy sickle, and reap:
for the time is come for thee to reap;
for the harvest of the earth is ripe."

16 And he that sat on the cloud thrust in his sickle on the
earth; and

the earth was reaped.

17 And another angel came out of the temple which is in
heaven, he also having a sharp sickle.

18 And another angel came out from the altar, which had
power over fire; and cried with a loud cry to him that had
the sharp sickle, saying,

"Thrust in thy sharp sickle,
and gather the clusters of the vine of the earth;
for her grapes are fully ripe."

19 And the angel thrust in his sickle into the earth, and

gathered the vine of the earth, and
cast it into the great winepress of the wrath of God.

20 And **the winepress was trodden without the city**, and
blood came out of the winepress, even unto the horse
bridles, by the space of a thousand and six hundred
furlongs.

View from Mount Sion
Christ's Solution

Rev. 14
It is impossible to be standing on the sand of the sea and on Mount Sion at the same time. The two environments are separated by a great gulf, as were Dives in hell and Lazarus in Abraham's bosom (see Luke 16:19–31). The sand of the sea is the dragon's lair filled with evil, deceit, and great turmoil; in contrast, Mount Sion is the harmony of a heaven filled with joy and light. Mount Sion is resurrection consciousness: the mental environment in which sin and hypocrisy do not exist and death is suspended.

From the summit where "all things are possible unto [God]" (Mark 14:36), we are about to witness Christ's solution: the new, perfect man is caught up unto God, being received as a little child, and the old concept of man is reaped, which separates fiction from fact in the minds of mortals. Since Mount Sion was John's view when he transcribed this text, we can deduce that it is possible to experience resurrection consciousness here on earth, just as he did. We may think that we will never be able to reach the heights of Jesus and John, but this is not true. They are illustrating the divine method of pardon through the realization of the Comforter, showing what it means to bear the first fruits.

> Verily, verily, I say unto you, He that believeth on me, the works that I do shall he do also; and greater works than these shall he do; because I go unto my Father (John 14:12).

If you are ignorant of the Comforter and his messenger or hear the Word and refuse to follow it, you will suffer the consequences of that depraved state "till thou know that the most High ruleth in the kingdom of men" (Dan. 4:25).

These two contrary views do not represent a division of people whereby some make it into heaven and some are condemned to hell. They represent two opposite states of consciousness. Eventually, the mind that functions as a brain—seeing, hearing, and feeling with the senses—is dissolved, and the view from Mount Sion reigns and is all-inclusive.

1 **And I looked, and, lo, a Lamb stood on the mount Sion, and with him an hundred forty and four thousand, having his Father's name written in their foreheads.**

After the Lamb opened the sixth seal in chapter 6, there was a pause in the narrative in order to prophesy the sealing of the Father's name in the foreheads of the one hundred forty-four thousand. In that interim, the Comforter presented a LITTLE BOOK OPEN and a REED LIKE UNTO A ROD, which enabled the Woman to be clothed with the sun and to bring forth the man child. With this preparatory understanding, we are now ready to see how it is that the Father's name is written in our foreheads.

Christ as a Lamb stands as the translator of love-filled consciousness. Standing with him is the sum total of all those manifest ideas that God has given him. For the Lamb and for each one of us, heaven would not be heaven if something or someone were missing.

The number one hundred forty-four thousand is a figure used to magnify the importance of all-good presence. When Jesus was asked how many times we should forgive, he said, "seventy times seven." Now Mount Sion is occupied by a symbolic twelve thousand times twelve. Magnifying the number twelve by one thousand is also consistent with the one thousand years, or one day with the Lord in which we occupy this heaven.

2–3 **And I heard a voice from heaven, as the voice of many waters, and as the voice of a great thunder: and I heard the voice of harpers harping with their harps: And they sung as it were a new song before the throne, and before the four beasts, and the elders: and no man could learn that song but the hundred and forty and four thousand, which were redeemed from the earth.**

When all earth-based references are gone—the noise of enticing suggestion and the clutter of mistakes—we are awestruck by the grand harmony of a singular, focused message, and it is music to our ears. We discover that the parameters for living have changed. Paul clarifies it this way: "If any man be in Christ, he is a new creature: old things are passed away; behold, all things are become new" (2 Cor. 5:17). *New,* meaning primal and unadulterated, is a permanent condition; it is a continuous fresh quality seen from the Mount. As we scan this present heaven, we realize that Christ is there approving the song and directing the chorus, for God is not separate from manifestation and has exclusive rights to its publication.

We are published in heaven, and there is none else.

4 **These are they which were not defiled with women; for they are virgins. These are they which follow the Lamb whithersoever he goeth. These were redeemed from among men, being the firstfruits unto God and to the Lamb.**

The dust man, Adam, chose to break the Lord God's commandment and taste Eve's fruit offering. The Christ man is neither defined nor defiled with dust, for he is the Son of man conceived as new and forever present as new.

The realization that we are worthy to be made "*like* unto the Son" of man is made possible through the Lamb's example. Those who begin with a pure heart and do not waver when temptation comes are the first fruits.

5 **And in their mouth was found no guile: for they are without fault before the throne of God.**

Jesus declared, "I do nothing of myself; but as my Father hath taught me, I speak these things" (John 8:28). When Christ moves the mouth, it cannot possibly be faulty.

6–7 **And I saw another angel fly in the midst of heaven, having the everlasting gospel to preach unto them that dwell on the earth, and to every nation, and kindred, and tongue, and people, Saying with a loud voice, Fear God, and give glory to him; for the hour of his judgment is come: and worship him that made heaven, and earth, and the sea, and the fountains of waters.**

Christ meets us where we are, speaks our language, takes us by the hand, and lifts us up. We then recognize the Comforter drawing us from above, renewing the message, and fulfilling the man. Paul heard it this way: "Come out from among them, and be ye separate, saith the Lord, and touch not the unclean thing; and I will receive you, And will be a Father unto you, and ye shall be my sons and daughters, saith the Lord Almighty" (2 Cor. 6:17–18).

The voice of conscience is perpetual, and righteous judgment rewards our practice according to our motives until we behold our home and heaven.

8 **And there followed another angel, saying, Babylon is fallen, is fallen, that great city, because she made all nations drink of the wine of the wrath of her fornication.**

> Every kingdom divided against itself is brought to desolation; and every city or house divided against itself shall not stand (Matt 12:25).

Babylon is built on the sand that made Adam mortal and susceptible to acting out sin. Practicing evil must, by definition, destroy both mind and body in the house or city of oneself.

Repetition of the text is not incidental: "Is fallen, is fallen" emphasizes the same two stages of cleansing that we have been witnessing all along. Babylon is defined by the belief in a power opposed to God and is the product of that belief. We must lose both mortal mind and mortal body: the *image of the beast* and the *beast* must fall before the light of Truth.

9–10 **And the third angel followed them, saying with a loud voice, If any man worship the beast and his image, and receive his mark in his forehead, or in his hand, The same shall drink of the wine of the wrath of God, which is poured out without mixture into the cup of his indignation; and he shall be tormented with fire and brimstone in the presence of the holy angels, and in the presence of the Lamb:**

Is there a contest going on between Christ and Satan, vying for control of our minds? No, this is impossible! Mind, God, is omnipotent, and Satan is ignorant of God. The mistaken premise is that we each have a mind that is subject to the influence of either Christ or Satan. Since there is no mind separate from God, the contest resides in our belief that we each have a mind.

Suppose you are in a deep sleep having a nightmare when a fire breaks out in your house. When the intensity of the heat and smoke wakes you from your dream, you see the damage to your house and feel the tragedy of your loss, but should not you be grateful, also, that the fire and brimstone woke you from the dream and saved your life? The intense inspiration of Christ wakes us from the dream of a power opposed to God. Fire and brimstone sound the alarm.

11 **And the smoke of their torment ascendeth up for ever and ever: and they have no rest day nor night, who worship the beast and his image, and whosoever receiveth the mark of his name.**

Why do we worship a body that God did not make? We all must ascend from the worship of body and mind to a higher awareness of good. Wherever we are on the path that leads heavenward, conscience is a constant torment to our sins until we stop sinning.

> I will not leave you comfortless: I will come to you (John 14:18).

12 **Here is the patience of the saints: here are they that keep the commandments of God, and the faith of Jesus.**

The Lamb will persist until all the lost sheep are found, for we are worthy. Every law of God that the saints have ever uttered will remain in some form until we find ourselves one with the saints and Christ.

13 **And I heard a voice from heaven saying unto me, Write, Blessed are the dead which die in the Lord from henceforth: Yea, saith the Spirit, that they may rest from their labours; and their works do follow them.**

John was convinced that the law of redemption would have to be recorded in our foreheads. Mental redemption requires that we die to all of evil's means and methods. The necessity to set aside physical sense is the basis of the first Beatitude and the inspiration for the crucifixion. Then the blessings come in a transformation of consciousness, and we walk forth with joy as Jesus demonstrated by his resurrection. When the struggle to hear God (and the tribulation felt for not hearing) is over, an abiding rest settles on us, for we have proven the Word by our works.

> He hath made his wonderful works to be remembered (Ps. 111:4).

14 **And I looked, and behold a white cloud, and upon the cloud one sat like unto the Son of man, having on his head a golden crown, and in his hand a sharp sickle.**

This is what the redeemed man looks like: a nous consciousness no longer laboring to hear God, set with royal authority and crowned with dominion. The white cloud indicates a pure sense of substance that is ready to be clarified as soon as that substance is demonstrated completely. It is a state of consciousness that is lifted up beyond physical law. The cloud will clear when the observer of the vision, having reaped for others what he had previously harvested out of himself, assumes his place on the throne, where the one "like unto the Son of man" belongs. The white cloud disappears at the ascension.

15 **And another angel came out of the temple, crying with a loud voice to him that sat on the cloud, Thrust in thy sickle, and reap: for the time is come for thee to reap; for the harvest of the earth is ripe.**

Resurrection consciousness prophesies and inspires universal salvation from the earth dream.

16 **And he that sat on the cloud thrust in his sickle on the earth; and the earth was reaped.**

After his resurrection, Jesus was able to take his sharp sickle and reap all mankind from the slavery of its false beliefs. Reaping the earth does not involve overcoming all the trials of the flesh for every individual. Jesus did not do this. As he saw God's manifestations individually alive to Spirit, Jesus could truthfully say, "Be of good cheer; I have overcome the world" (John 16:33) because he could no longer see evil in those individuals. Jesus saw all mankind awakened from the mortal dream.

The Christ idea has been preparing mankind for the sickle in every verse of the Apocalypse:

- First, the churches' inadequacies were separated from their works: "He that hath an ear, let him hear."
- Second, Christ broke the seals that were preventing man from knowing the original meaning of Scripture.
- Third, the angels separated the physical and mental nature of sin from man.
- Fourth, the Comforter opened our blind eyes.
- Fifth, our eyes beheld the Woman and the man child (the *co-incidence* that the Comforter brings).
- Sixth, the view from the sand of the sea exposed the chaff of lust and hypocrisy.
- Seventh, the way was cleared for us to behold the view from Mount Sion, which set the parameters for universal salvation.

17 **And another angel came out of the temple which is in heaven, he also having a sharp sickle.**

One sickle reaps from the white cloud that is present and visible from earth while the other reaps from heaven. This is consistent with the Christ—which comes to earthly consciousness to destroy our belief in sin, sickness, and death—and with the Comforter, which never leaves heaven for earth but draws from above. This angel message has emerged from the temple of perfection to illustrate and fulfill a divine purpose.

18–19 **And another angel came out from the altar, which had power over fire; and cried with a loud cry to him that had the sharp sickle, saying, Thrust in thy sharp sickle, and gather the clusters of the vine of the earth; for her grapes are fully ripe. And the angel thrust in his sickle into the earth, and gathered the vine of the earth, and cast it into the great winepress of the wrath of God.**

The angel from the altar reminds us of the spiritual purgation (baptism by fire) in chapters 8 and 9, which prepared us to manifest God's priesthood.

From the vantage point of the angel and the "one like unto the Son of man," the reaping is a glorious event because the blood (spiritual life) and wine (inspiration of Love) are separated permanently from the lie and the liar. From the vantage point of the one being reaped, it may feel like being trampled in a winepress.

20 **And the winepress was trodden without the city, and blood came out of the winepress, even unto the horse bridles, by the space of a thousand and six hundred furlongs.**

Only the pure in heart reside in the consciousness of perfect harmony. The separation of fact from fable must occur outside the city's boundaries. Michael and his angels do the holy work of treading sin and hypocrisy out of us so that the precious lifeblood, the inspiration of love, can be self-seen and acknowledged.

Although this winepress is designed to save us from ourselves when all other methods have failed, mortal man does not welcome it. Sixteen hundred furlongs equals two million steps and is equivalent to approximately one hundred eighty-nine miles (304 km). *Furlong* means furrow length and was first used to measure a plowed field, which brings to mind the verse in Ezekiel 21:27: "I will overturn, overturn, overturn, it: and it shall be no more, until he come whose right it is; and I will give it him." The product—blood and wine—is oneness with Life and Love. Consider that if any part of us refuses to acknowledge God, it may take two million stamping impressions to accept spiritual life and reject the lie of death. The winepress is prophetic of the so-called wrath of God and amounts to blessings not understood.

THE SEVEN VIALS

Rev 15–16

Rev. 15

1 And I saw another sign in heaven, great and marvellous,

SEVEN ANGELS
HAVING THE SEVEN LAST PLAGUES;
for in them is filled up the wrath of God.

2 And I saw as it were a **sea of glass** mingled with fire: and them that had gotten the victory

- over the beast, and
- over his image, and
- over his mark, and
- over the number of his name,

stand on the sea of glass, having the harps of God.

3 And they sing the

- song of Moses the servant of God, and the
- song of the Lamb, saying,

"Great and marvellous are thy works, Lord God Almighty; just and true are thy ways, thou King of saints.
4 Who shall not fear thee, O Lord, and glorify thy name? for thou only art holy: for all nations shall come and worship before thee; for thy judgments are made manifest."

5 And after that I looked, and, behold,

the temple
of the tabernacle of the testimony in heaven
was opened:

6 And the seven angels came out of the temple, having the seven plagues, **clothed in pure and white linen**, and having their breasts girded with **golden girdles**.

7 And one of the four beasts gave unto the seven angels

SEVEN GOLDEN VIALS
FULL OF THE WRATH OF GOD,
who liveth for ever and ever.

8 And the temple was filled with smoke from the glory of
God, and from his power; and no man was able to enter
into the temple, till the seven plagues of the seven
angels were fulfilled.

Rev. 16

1 And I heard a great voice out of the temple saying to the
seven angels, "Go your ways, and
pour out the vials of the wrath of God upon the earth."

2 And the **first** went, and poured out his vial upon the earth;
and there fell a noisome and grievous sore upon the men
which had the mark of the beast, and upon them which
worshipped his image.

3 And the **second angel** poured out his vial upon the sea; and
it became as the blood of a dead man: and every living soul
died in the sea.

4 And the **third angel** poured out his vial upon the rivers and
fountains of waters; and they became blood.

5 And I heard the angel of the waters say, "Thou art
righteous, O Lord, which art, and wast, and shalt be,
because thou hast judged thus.
6 For they have shed the blood of saints and prophets,
and thou hast given them blood to drink; for they are
worthy."

7 And I heard another out of the altar say,
"Even so, Lord God Almighty,
true and righteous are thy judgments."

8 And the **fourth angel** poured out his vial upon the sun; and
power was given unto him to scorch men with fire.
9 And men were scorched with great heat, and blasphemed
the name of God, which hath power over these plagues: and
they repented not to give him glory.

10 And the **fifth angel** poured out his vial upon the seat of the
beast; and his kingdom was full of darkness; and they
gnawed their tongues for pain,
11 And blasphemed the God of heaven because of their pains
and their sores, and repented not of their deeds.

12 And the **sixth angel** poured out his vial upon the great river
Euphrates; and the water thereof was dried up, that the way
of the kings of the east might be prepared.

13 And I saw three unclean spirits like frogs come

- out of the mouth of the **dragon**, and
- out of the mouth of the **beast**, and
- out of the mouth of the **false prophet**.

14 For they are the spirits of devils, working miracles,
which go forth unto the kings of the earth and of the
whole world, to gather them to the battle of that great
day of God Almighty.

15 "Behold, I come as a thief. Blessed is he that watcheth, and
keepeth his garments, lest he walk naked, and they see his
shame."

16 **And he gathered them together into a place called in the**
Hebrew tongue ARMAGEDDON.

17 And the **seventh angel** poured out his vial into the air; and
there came a great voice out of the temple of heaven, from
the throne, saying,

"IT IS DONE."

18 And there were voices, and thunders, and lightnings; and
there was a great earthquake, such as was not since men
were upon the earth, so mighty an earthquake, and so great.

19 And **the great city was divided into three parts**
and the cities of the nations fell: and great Babylon came in
remembrance before God, to give unto her the cup of the
wine of the fierceness of his wrath.
20 And every island fled away, and the mountains were not
found.
21 And there fell upon men a great hail out of heaven, every
stone about the weight of a talent:
and **men blasphemed God**
because of the plague of the hail;
for the plague thereof was exceeding great.

THE SEVEN VIALS—Armageddon is Upon Us!
Reaping the Earth and Vine

Rev. 15–16
As noted previously, the first half of Revelation chronicles man's step-by-step enlightenment based on a searching desire for it until he becomes fully aware of his identity as the perfect manifestation of God in chapter 12. Beginning in chapter 13, the sequence for attaining enlightenment is repeated from the standpoint of *defiance* of God rather than from a searching desire. Here is the pattern:

> S*ubmission* to the seven angels
> sounding reveals an OPEN BOOK
> and a REED LIKE A ROD.
>
> *Defiance* to the message of the seven
> vials produces ARMAGEDDON.
>
> *Consecration* to good reveals the
> dominion Woman clothed with the
> sun and the man child caught up
> unto God.
>
> D*efiance* produces the great whore
> and Babylon divided.

After the Comforter and its progeny are presented to us, will we reject them, just as we did Christ? Will we find Love and Truth difficult to swallow, and even more difficult to digest? Will we dilute the message ever so slightly to make it more palatable, or walk away pretending that we never heard it? Will we put off doing the work for a more convenient time? We must pay all for the pearl of great price, even our sense of life, for divine Life has no room for our personal concepts.

When Moses approached Pharaoh with God's demand to free the children of Israel from bondage, Pharaoh refused. He could not accept the power that Moses wielded with a rod of iron because it violated his personal sense of authority.

This refusal caused him to suffer great loss, the most important of which was his own salvation. Pharaoh knew that he was separate from Moses' God, but rather than change his ways, he hated Moses for revealing this fact. Pharaoh's anguish over his own powerlessness to fight God's way was his personal Armageddon, and the casting of the seven vials of the wrath of God is symbolic of what was happening to his earth domain. Wrath is not God's view nor the seven angels' view, for they are not suffering in the least. Jesus told Matthew, "They that take the sword shall perish with the sword" (Matt. 26:52).

When escaping the bondage of Egypt, the children of Israel could see the power of God that Moses wielded. As soon as they got hungry, however, they murmured against the path of freedom and would gladly have gone back to slavery rather than subsist in the desert. Moses chose the high path and talked with God. Most of the Israelites saw the miracles but chose the enslaved, earthly path that offered nothing but the shallow comfort of bread and a bed. In chapters 15 and 16, the entire narrative surrounding the wrath of God is written from the perspective of man clinging to earth in a hopeless attempt to justify sin.

Imagine, now, that through our own cleverness and a little cheating here and there, we have built nest eggs for ourselves: money, success, houses, families, and friends. Then all of a sudden, some evidence comes along that threatens to expose our underhanded methods, degrade our social status, and take away our inflated salaries. Even though we know we are guilty, would we fight to conceal the evidence in order to hold on to what we have acquired? This is Pharaoh mentality.

Now imagine another scenario. In this one we are doing everything right according to normal world thought. Our intelligence, dedication, and hard work have made us accomplished, recognized, and respected by our peers.

We have learned to live by the world's standards and accept them as valid. Then along comes a Christ thought that provides true understanding of Jesus' message, and we look around and see that everything we have striven for was in vain. We are standing in the place where Solomon declared, "Then I looked on all the works that my hands had wrought, and on the labour that I had laboured to do: and, behold, all was vanity and vexation of spirit, and there was no profit under the sun" (Eccl. 2:11). Is not there a temptation in the human mind to conceal the evidence of the Comforter and to keep the world thought of which we are so addicted? This is the battle that we all must lose, for God has power over these addictions and will see us safely home, even though we find ourselves kicking and screaming all the way. The plagues and wrath of God that we are about to witness are suffering humanity's views, blood-ridden from sin and hypocrisy.

In the previous two chapters, the great distance between the dragon's lair and the view from Mount Sion was identified. The battle lines are drawn, and it is impossible to find any compromise between infinite Love and the void of hatred. **Armageddon is upon us!** The two sickles are ready to sever our addiction to *good and evil*. We cannot have these. Armageddon is suicide for both sinner and sin.

When mankind looks toward heaven while still clinging to earth, the certainty of sin, disease, and death stands in total defiance of divine possibilities. God is even blamed for allowing or perpetuating these plagues. However, it is our erroneous perceptions that taint all the evidence reaching man. The purpose of the seven vials is not to destroy man but to destroy the device that is causing the error. We are about to witness error divided against itself. The amalgamation of good and evil does not coexist as a thought or as a thing called man; insofar as we believe it does, we will suffer the consequences of that belief.

Rev. 15

1 **And I saw another sign in heaven, great and marvellous, seven angels having the seven last plagues; for in them is filled up the wrath of God.**

John, standing in resurrection consciousness, understood what was once a mystery. To him, the angels stood for victory over evil, and it was a marvelous sight, but he also understood how those very angels plague mortal man's mental and physical domain with evidence contrary to their inclinations. At Jesus' birth, Joseph intuitively sensed the threat to the babe's life and confounded Herod's intent to harm him. Herod, the cruelest form of mortal man, saw the angelic birth as a threat to his throne. From his perspective, God's wrath was upon him, and he chose to attack that threat.

To know why the seven pure angels have the seven last plagues in the first place is to understand why error appears to exist but is not real. Remember, this is mortal man's concept of those angels; it is not the angels' concept of themselves. To a murderer, the evidence that an eyewitness holds is a plague to him, for it has the power to cast him into prison. Likewise, these angels have the evidence to convict our faults.

2 **And I saw as it were a sea of glass mingled with fire: and them that had gotten the victory over the beast, and over his image, and over his mark, and over the number of his name, stand on the sea of glass, having the harps of God.**

In order for John to observe this vista, he had to be sitting on the throne at one with Christ. This vision eclipses material law. What appeared to be dark and mysterious as viewed from the sand of the sea is now transparent.

A sea of glass mingled with fire would melt sand back together, restoring it to one whole. In addition, molten glass is almost a universal solvent. So it is in this metaphor that all error is dissolved in the infinite sea of divine Love. The children of God clearly understand and utilize the structure of Truth and Love; they stand before John and Christ, ready to sing. Tired humanity, however, reads the verses but is not prepared; to mankind, perfection is an unattainable ideal that is not worth attempting. Ask someone if he can walk on water, and he may snicker and say, 'Of course not!' rather than respond with the more hopeful statement, 'Not yet.'

3 **And they sing the song of Moses the servant of God, and the song of the Lamb, saying, Great and marvellous are thy works, Lord God Almighty; just and true are thy ways, thou King of saints.**

To sing the song of Moses and the Lamb is to be on the same plane as they are, no longer followers of holy men but fellow musicians in the chorus. Those who have attained the victory know that they are not guilty, but to the stubborn human mind, the song of Moses and the Lamb is a death knell because self-will is riddled with guilt.

4 **Who shall not fear thee, O Lord, and glorify thy name? for thou only art holy: for all nations shall come and worship before thee; for thy judgments are made manifest.**

Reverent obedience to Truth and Love allows one to recognize the glory of all existence. As good is universal, ever grateful, and naturally expressing itself, so the manifestation of good—you and I—must improve our ideals until no other conclusion is possible.

5 **And after that I looked, and, behold, the temple of the tabernacle of the testimony in heaven was opened:**

The veil of Moses' temple in the wilderness was rent from top to bottom; John had entered the Holy of Holies. In other words, John saw ignorance removed from consciousness.

What he had previously thought were secrets of God had become the truth of being. John had now proven for himself the words of the Master and was worthy to be called a true disciple of Christ.

6 **And the seven angels came out of the temple, having the seven plagues, clothed in pure and white linen, and having their breasts girded with golden girdles.**

Every idea emitted from God carries its own pure and perfect evidence of the all-seeing Mind, yet we face spiritual scrutiny with apprehension. The angels who have come out to inform and enlighten are seen as having plagues whose purpose it is to torment, for we know our mistakes will be exposed.

7 **And one of the four beasts gave unto the seven angels seven golden vials full of the wrath of God, who liveth for ever and ever.**

Omnipotence, omniscience, omnipresence, and omni-action—working together as one—give the consecrated messengers the means by which to deliver truth to man. The so-called wrath of God is really the unction of spiritual causation delivered to our doorstep by Christ.

8 **And the temple was filled with smoke from the glory of God, and from his power; and no man was able to enter into the temple, till the seven plagues of the seven angels were fulfilled.**

Man's greatest fear has now assumed its final form. Anxiety over the unknown, ignorance of God, and the general fear of death are supplanted—now man is no longer ignorant. He knows his ways and means are wrong, but he is addicted to himself. Standing in willful self-guilt and pulling the veil over his own face, he hopes to pass by unnoticed because he is terrified of the punishment for defying the Comforter, Christ, and God. Hiding in the void of his own earth cave, man prays for something that will prevent his nakedness from being exposed. He knows that the smoke of his own mind's excuses is lethal, yet he refuses to give up his fantasies.

Rev. 16

We have seen the seven plagues before in chapters 8 and 9, where the seven angels sounded their trumpets during the baptism by fire, but now we are looking from a different perspective. In the earlier examination, humbled man voluntarily laid himself on the altar and survived, partly because he was willing to be baptized. This time we examine the consequences of a man living in the post OPEN-BOOK epoch, who is still trying to conquer his fears all by himself and refuses to demonstrate what the OPEN BOOK implies—a premise that must prove fatal.

> Unto every one that hath shall be given, and he shall have abundance: but from him that hath not shall be taken away even that which he hath. And cast ye the unprofitable servant into outer darkness: there shall be weeping and gnashing of teeth (Matt. 25:29–30).

Saul of Tarsus was a first-class Torah scholar; he may have had it memorized. His intelligence, and strong will intent on preserving Judaism, framed his personality. Unfortunately, Saul was stuck in the stricture of the letter. He could not see the inspired Christ message that Scripture recorded until the moment arrived when he saw how Jesus' acts fulfilled the ancient prophecies. The truth of Jesus' words and deeds overwhelmed him, making apparent his own blindness to Christ during all those years of study. *He saw that he had been blind to Christ, and now that blindness was felt.* Jesus said, "I will shew him how great things he must suffer for my name's sake" (Acts 9:16). For three days, Saul sat in anguish until faithful Ananias saw through the mask of error, and his eyes reopened with a new kind of spiritual clarity. Once we grasp this mental pattern, we will see it repeated throughout Scripture and in ourselves every day.

God did not make Paul suffer. Christ caused him to be introspective—to see a picture of his own mental state. The pain Paul felt was the result of his temporary unwillingness to leave the old letter for the new OPEN BOOK. The unprepared children of Israel suffered for 400 years in Egypt and for 40 more years in the wilderness, not because God was unavailable but because they were not listening. They lived the results of their enslaved thoughts and fears until they abandoned them. So do we.

When we realize that our experience is a direct result of the mental picture we entertain, we will stop trying to fix the *thing* and start healing the *thought* that produced it. Rather than exchanging a bad belief for a better belief, revelatory healing requires giving up belief entirely in exchange for the embodiment of "one like unto the Son of man"—one who is living directly in the light and harmony of God.

Mortal man's ways and means have been ingrained in the fabric of our earthly existence since the beginning of time. When we come face to face with fulfilled prophecy and find it to be completely contrary to our compulsions, it sends a shock wave through our sense of what is normal and right. We cannot deny the OPEN BOOK anymore than Saul could deny Jesus, but we temporarily cling to our mistakes and suffer accordingly, just as Saul did. God's Word written in our foreheads will always be rejected by minds inscribed with lies. It is time for that error-filled vessel to be replaced with new wine and a new bottle—perfect Mind and perfect manifestation. This chapter is a picture of the old vessel that hears the Comforter and rejects it. The fruit is gathered and trodden in the winepress (Rev. 14:18–20). In spite of objections, the force of divine Truth and Love causes the lie to be self-seen.

> Watch with me (Matt 26:38).
>
> But they refused to hearken, and pulled away the shoulder, and stopped their ears, that they should not hear. . . . Thus the land was desolate after them, that no man passed through nor returned: for they laid the pleasant land desolate (Zech. 7:11, 14).

Rev. 16

1 **And I heard a great voice out of the temple saying to the seven angels, Go your ways, and pour out the vials of the wrath of God upon the earth.**

Like John, we all must come to acknowledge our wholly spiritual source and wholly spiritual identity. However, the pathway to achieving that goal is strewn with questions, anxieties, a sensual body, and all the pains and pleasures associated with sin and hypocrisy. Success is, nonetheless, inevitable because Truth is real, and Christ has provided the means. Like it or not, awake or asleep, the first evidence of Christ is a conscience, and that conscience is relentless; it will not go away. Truth is poured out!

> Behold, I stand at the door, and knock: if any man hear my voice, and open the door, I will come in to him, and will sup with him, and he with me (Rev. 3:20).

Christ's coaxing presence is a powerful force, but it is also a nuisance to a mind filled with contraries. As each vial in the sequence pours out convincing evidence of God, we find man screaming his objections because admitting the truth is contrary to both physical law and mental inclinations. As man delves more deeply into the mystery of human existence and opposes the advancing spiritual ideas, the futility of his war with truth becomes increasingly apparent.

The following text represents the type of inner warfare that we might have in our minds as these vials are poured out one by one.

2 **And the first went, and poured out his vial upon the earth; and there fell a noisome and grievous sore upon the men which had the mark of the beast, and upon them which worshipped his image.**

Earth defined materially is body, individually and collectively; earth defined spiritually is home, heaven.

First Vial: 'Matter does not identify or circumscribe man.'

Darkness: 'When I was with you in the Garden, I was surrounded with good. All my desires were simple and easily fulfilled with one glance around me. In breaking your commandment not to eat from the tree of good and evil, I felt exposed to all kinds of wants, opinions, choices, and desires that I hadn't thought of before. It was as if a wall of darkness went up in front of me, and I was outside your grace.'

Self-knowledge: 'I was given a body and assumed it to be real. It was not my idea. I awoke on this earth as a sentient, self-conscious creature, confined in and looking out from a physical body. My senses have allowed me to navigate and collect information. Whatever I retain defines my existence, and the choices I make describe my personality. Unfortunately, my senses are limited, my memory is faulty, and my choices sometimes get me into trouble. I pursue physical pleasure for its enticing benefits, but all my fancied joys fade: they do not last as I imagined they would. The constant threat of lack, loss, and pain induces stress, which in turn increases the possibility of the very plagues I fear. As I look around at my life here, I conclude that I am ultimately doomed to die. This plague is a grievous sore.'

Desire: 'I desperately want to find my way back, to be with you again.'

Grief: 'It hurts being so alone, so threatened, so hopelessly desperate.'

Wrath: 'How could you do this to me? Why don't you help?'

Reluctant Humanity: 'Are you declaring that I must give up everything that I know about *me*—all concern and awareness of my physical body—so that I may understand my body as God sees me? Why do you ask such a thing? Comfort me, forgive my sins, and heal my diseases—take care of me right here. Do not tell me that I must lose my sense of self!'

The apostle Thomas easily associated Christ with bodily evidence, but affirming spiritual evidence was more difficult for him: "Except I shall see in his hands the print of the nails, and put my finger into the print of the nails, and thrust my hand into his side, I will not believe" (John 20:25).

3 **And the second angel poured out his vial upon the sea; and it became as the blood of a dead man: and every living soul died in the sea.**

On the one hand, the sea suggests something in motion, a swirling mixture of many minds from which all animated matter is presumed to have evolved; on the other, a sea of glass radiates a living stillness where creation is seen as complete and in perfect order. Whatever theories are false regarding the sea cannot survive the scrutiny of truth.

Second Vial: 'Life (God) evolves man.'

Darkness: 'Outside the Garden, I feel almost completely separate from God and lost in the dark cave of my own skull, desperately trying to find my way back home.'

Ignorance: 'I have no idea where I came from or where I am going.'

Self-knowledge: 'I can trace my evolution from protoplasm to fish, to monkeys, to man. Coincidental molecular attraction found successes and reproduced itself; however, when I follow the trail of evolution past the one-celled life form into complex chemistry, I run into a dead end. I have never been able to figure out why anatomical life begins, why it multiplies, and why it dies. It's still a mystery, but I know this: God has nothing to do with the form I know as man. Survival of the fittest made me, and in my weakness, I will become extinct!'

Second Vial: 'You are correct in this regard: God has nothing to do with the form *you know* as man. "Before Abraham was, I am"' (John 8:58).

Reluctant Humanity: 'Are you implying that I should struggle to negate my ancestry as inconsequential in order that Christ may show me a spiritual lineage that has no beginning? How can I see beyond what the eyes can behold?'

Attachment to Body: 'My human origin may be dubious, but it is less transcendental than man in the image and likeness of God. To say that life existed before I knew anything about it and that it was complete without any help from the sea-incubator process is to deny all the fossil evidence and my own body. For millennia genetics has fashioned my family tree, and I accept both the good and the bad of it. My mind cannot grasp Jesus' statement, "Before Abraham was, I am."'

Wrath: 'I hate your blatant, mysterious answers. Are you intentionally confusing me just to make me squirm?'

Self-justification: 'God must be a careless parent; otherwise, I would already know from whence I came.'

When Peter was drowning in a sea of self-doubt and confusion concerning Jesus' pending crucifixion, he betrayed him three times. When approached by witnesses, he swore, "I know not what thou sayest. . . . I do not know the man. . . . I know not the man. And immediately the cock crew. . . . And he went out, and wept bitterly" (Matt. 26:70–75).

4 **And the third angel poured out his vial upon the rivers and fountains of waters; and they became blood.**

Looking deeper into the law of opposites, we find that the mental and physical cause underlying human means and methods is in stark contrast to the river of Life. Life poured out spiritually nullifies the lifeblood associated with material living.

Third Vial: 'Life is God. I am your lifeblood.'

Darkness: 'I am trying to be still in my earth-cave body and pray for guidance, but my mind is wandering and my heart is pounding; my life has no direction or purpose.'

Craving: 'Just give me something to do, a place to be, and someone to love me so that I can ignore the irreconcilable differences between matter and Spirit.'

Self-knowledge: 'I carry the essentials of my sea origin within my blood, and I am a successful organic mechanism. Matter and energy are all there is to my universe. Atoms form the elements of which I am made. Hydrogen, oxygen, carbon, etcetera compose the man I call me. All this being said, it is hard to fathom the idea that I came from nothing; that all action and reaction in physics will eventually come to a halt; and that however fascinating, beautiful, and complex my universe is, the stream of life and matter will eventually disappear.'

Third Vial: 'Your stream of life disappears because "in the beginning God created the heaven and the earth. And the earth was *without* form, and void" (Gen. 1:1–2). In other words, it was complete without matter. In Principle, matter never had substance or origin. My real creation is permanent. False, imagined creations have no abiding place.'

> All the host of heaven shall be dissolved, and the heavens shall be rolled together as a scroll: and all their host shall fall down, as the leaf falleth off from the vine, and as a falling fig from the fig tree (Isa. 34:4).

Reluctant Humanity: 'To say that matter never had substance or origin is to tell me that there never was any life in matter. How can I become aware of an idea without being physically alive? Without blood and brains, I would not even be able to contemplate an idea.'

Wrath: 'See me! Touch me! Smell me! This body and its life story are real and overwhelming evidence that I cannot deny. Why are you tormenting me with knowledge of a spiritual life source that I can neither adopt nor adapt to my present circumstance? I cannot leave my earthly connections and solid convictions to follow Christ. I worship myself.'

After John the Baptist was put in prison, he questioned whether Jesus was the Messiah. "Among those that are born of women there is not a greater prophet than John the Baptist: but he that is least in the kingdom of God is greater than he" (Luke 7:28).

5–6 **And I heard the angel of the waters say, Thou art righteous, O Lord, which art, and wast, and shalt be, because thou hast judged thus. For they have shed the blood of saints and prophets, and thou hast given them blood to drink; for they are worthy.**

At the same time that mortal man is arguing with himself—bewildered by a maze of self-importance, self-justification, and guilt—he is being pressed to adopt the evidence presented by conscience, intuition, and grace. We suffer and die, bearing the fruit of our own mistakes until we stop making them. Self-inflicted trials have nothing to do with our real worth.

7 **And I heard another out of the altar say, Even so, Lord God Almighty, true and righteous are thy judgments.**

Truth is always ready. Trying to destroy the blood (life) of the Lamb is futile. Conscience and guilt will haunt us until we accept divine life and live it. The human mind tries to block all avenues of budding inspiration, but eventually Christ opens the way to spiritual consciousness. Then our worthiness is witnessed and acknowledged as we realize our own true reflection: "I am one that bear witness of myself, and the Father that sent me beareth witness of me" (John 8:18).

8–9 **And the fourth angel poured out his vial upon the sun; and power was given unto him to scorch men with fire. And men were scorched with great heat, and blasphemed the name of God, which hath power over these plagues: and they repented not to give him glory.**

Is the sun a primal energy source from which all life is derived, or is omnipotent Mind the only creative intelligence? Neither acknowledges, accommodates, nor compromises any position with the other: "Let God be true, but every man a liar" (Rom. 3:4).

Fourth Vial: 'I am the light of the World—I (Christ, Truth) manifest all there is to your real life as sons and daughters of God. It is the energy of divine Life that animates you, and there is no other power.'

Darkness: 'I have read Holy Scripture, listened to sermons, bowed my head, repeated my prayers, declared my sins, sang in the choir, and done everything I am supposed to do; still, I sit here in the dark. I don't really know what any of it means. I have never felt connected beyond my own imagination. Deep inside, I feel alone. My health is failing, and I am in pain. I am doing the best I know and am getting nowhere. My house is on fire, and death is at the door.'

Self-knowledge: 'My life proceeded from the big bang. The universe is teeming with energy, and we are in the perfect spot in time and space to benefit from it. Change the parameters ever so slightly, and we will be annihilated. We are very lucky at the moment, though fate is against us. I worry about that sometimes, but not today.'

Reluctant Humanity: 'To say there is no power apart from God is to say that all the power of my universe is impotent. Are you insisting that I stop what I am doing and wait to be moved by divine light? I won't. The price is too high, and I'm too busy.'

Wrath: 'I hate your Mind directive. If I follow your path, I will lose *my* way, *my* universe, and *my* body. To me, that is death!'

10–11 **And the fifth angel poured out his vial upon the seat of the beast; and his kingdom was full of darkness; and they gnawed their tongues for pain, And blasphemed the God of heaven because of their pains and their sores, and repented not of their deeds.**

Anything that would attempt to usurp the throne of God is the seat of the beast. Digging beneath the subjective sense of matter, we find a bottomless pit of hypnotic mental suggestion offering a personal ego, a physical body, sensual pleasures, a mind full of arguing opposites, and a gradual decline into chaos, pain, and death. To the mind caught up in such a dream, this depressing state is all there is. But the fifth angel pours out the contents of the Mind of God. Christ and the Comforter are the teachers that wake up the dreamer and dissolve the dream. For many of us, we do not make this transition willingly: we cling to the error even as it is being destroyed, suffering terribly from the losses that are required for our own awakening.

Fifth Vial: 'All is Mind, God. Matter and mortal body have no intelligence; you sit on *My* throne as *My* idea.'

Darkness: 'Having the OPEN BOOK readily available is not what I thought it would be. I expected that surely Jesus would come to me, forgive all my sins, wipe away my tears, restore my body, and give me a mansion in heaven because I said to him, "I accept you as my Lord and Savior." I didn't realize I was going to have to actually do all the things he told me to be mindful of, before I would even be worthy of being called a disciple. It's impossible—a catch twenty-two. If I don't do it, I die, and if I do what is demanded, I voluntarily give up my sense of life. Tell me again: what is required?'

Fifth Vial: '"Do not commit adultery, Do not kill, Do not steal, Do not bear false witness, Defraud not, Honour thy father and mother. . . . sell whatsoever thou hast, and give to the poor, . . . take up the cross, and follow me" (Mark 10:19, 21).

'"Heal the sick, cleanse the lepers, raise the dead, cast out devils: freely ye have received, freely give" (Matt. 10:8).

"'Be ye therefore perfect, even as your Father which is in heaven is perfect'" (Matt. 5:48).

Evil Resistance: 'All that I call *me* and everything that I own is part of the grand scheme of things, which have nothing to do with God, the Commandments, or spiritual wisdom. I refuse to sell all that I have, and I will not listen. I have a mind. I think for myself. I will keep all of my pleasures, my sweet dreams, and my adventures. I am fascinated by the intrigue of fear. Mystery, contests, and contrary opinions are part of the game that keeps life interesting. Innocence and being of one Mind must be terribly boring.'

Ignorance: 'If God knows everything, then he knows I am weak, yet he does nothing about it. If he truly loved me, he would relieve my stresses and aches and pains. I don't think he has heard a word I have said.'

Self-indulgent Mental Power: 'I have discovered that my thoughts have a profound effect on my body and circumstances. If I change my thought, my universe accommodates in a significant way. I am now super aware of the power of my thoughts, and I manipulate my world in accordance with my wishes. Unfortunately, bad energy can hurt me just as much as good energy can help. I am terrified that sooner or later I will fall victim to my worst nightmares: "That which I was afraid of is come unto me"' (Job 3:25).

Reluctant Humanity: 'To say that God, Mind, is all is to exclude the thought forces that trace the universe upon the cranium. How can I, as a human, even think of God when you say that there is no power in brain to absorb the idea? I have heard that Jesus healed, and taught others to heal through their thoughtful prayers. Whose mind is doing that healing? Science says impossibilities never occur, but these events defy physics and common sense. Jesus' accomplishments make mine look minuscule.'

Wrath: 'Healing is not only God's domain! I, too, can diagnose disease and fix it. My way requires no moral cleansing and no prayer. Yes, my methods are tentative and experimental and not as successful as I would like them to be. As soon as I can find a way to eliminate diseases faster than new ones are discovered, I will have solved the riddle. When I do that, there will be no need for people to seek God.'

Lethal jealousy tries in vain to wipe out Mind. Jealous Cain, the first child of Adam, killed his brother Abel. Since that time, mankind has witnessed the transformative power of Mind as demonstrated by Jesus and his followers; nevertheless, we still reject the spiritual impetuous they presented, suffering greatly as a result. The by-product of jealousy is agony.

12–14 **And the sixth angel poured out his vial upon the great river Euphrates; and the water thereof was dried up, that the way of the kings of the east might be prepared. And I saw three unclean spirits like frogs come out of the mouth of the dragon, and out of the mouth of the beast, and out of the mouth of the false prophet. For they are the spirits of devils, working miracles, which go forth unto the kings of the earth and of the whole world, to gather them to the battle of that great day of God Almighty.**

According to Genesis 2, Euphrates was the fourth and final river to flow out from Eden; therefore, it contained all the ingredients of humanity's original home and defined its boundaries. Drying up Euphrates removes man's sanguine hope of ever finding his way back to Eden and a state of finite bliss.

Euphrates, defined spiritually, is the Comforter—the omniscience of man and the universe. The primal currents of Truth and Love that cannot be dried up are the OPEN BOOK and a REED LIKE UNTO A ROD. This angel is drying up our conception of humanity so that God's conception of man as image and likeness will be the only option available. This divine sense of Euphrates represents the original and final solution, the open passage that brings knowledge of salvation to humanity, thus drawing us back home—to Spirit.

The kings of the east are now prepared to work their magic so that their secret and peculiar treasures can be exposed and denounced. Unlike the three wise men of the East, who were willing to offer up their treasures for the true Messiah, these kings are not submitting. They are preparing to battle the day of God Almighty and to use their incantations to deceive "the kings of the earth and of the whole world." These unclean magi cannot destroy man because they have no such power, so they attempt to lure him with distractions to keep him from searching for his inheritance as a child of God.

Frogs are like Satan in that they do not exhibit any conscience at all. They will consume anything they can get in their mouths, including each other. Metaphorically, "unclean spirits like frogs" may refer to toad venom, which contains several poisons that have some nasty effects: two are psychedelic; one creates an erratic heart beat; one destroys heart tissue; one is adrenaline that increases heart rate and the fight or flight response of a sympathetic nervous system; one is a stress hormone; and one is serotonin that affects the gut (digestion), mood, appetite, sleep, muscle contraction, memory, learning, and blood clotting. This venom is seen coming out of the mouths of the dragon, the beast, and the false prophet. We recognize these three.

The dragon is a bloated version of the serpent in Genesis 2. It is the belief in a power opposed to God. When we accept or indulge in a power other than good, the villainous effects of the beast and the false prophet have ready ingress into our experience. The beast is the material body and the physical senses. The false prophet is the evil that animates the beast. This is the stage in which lust and hypocrisy play out the dream of a mortal's mind opposed to the Comforter. Here, in accordance with one's thoughts, it is possible to love and get it wrong, to think and miss the mark, to accumulate vast quantities of material wealth and have nothing of value, and to be happy and content sometimes but miserable and sick at other times. By perverse dissuasion, the beast and the false prophet will try every tactic known to block the conscious realization of our true being. Eventually the weapons used by evil collapse upon themselves, and man walks free of those burdens.

Sixth Vial: 'This promise has been fulfilled in your ears: "I will pray the Father, and he shall give you another Comforter, that he may abide with you for ever; Even the Spirit of truth; whom the world cannot receive, because it seeth him not, neither knoweth him: but ye know him; for he dwelleth with you, and shall be in you" (John 14:16–17). "But whosoever shall deny me before men, him will I also deny before my Father which is in heaven"' (Matt. 10:33).

'The knowing presence of divine Love is the simple and profound answer that was, and is, and shall be poured out upon you continually. Love is the alpha and omega of your being. Love is the river of life that has followed you here and will see you safely home. The Spirit of truth is Love understood and lived. Without My love, you have no protection. Without Love, evil would have ready access to you. Without Love, there would be no definition, no order, no understanding, no beauty, no law, no power, no light, and no life. Love is the embrace that encircles every idea of God from the infinitesimal to the infinite.'

Dragon: 'Kill the messenger!'

Lethal Jealousy: '"It is expedient for us, that one man should die for the people, and that the whole nation perish not"' (John 11:50).

Guile: '"Judas Iscariot, went unto the chief priests, And said unto them, What will ye give me, and I will deliver him unto you?"' (Matt. 26:14–15).

Now this man purchased a field with the reward of iniquity; and falling headlong, he burst asunder in the midst, and all his bowels gushed out (Acts 1:18).

Judas best exemplified what happens when we hate the Comforter. Lust and hypocrisy become so blatant that even Judas was forced to admit his heinous crime against Christ and waiting humanity: "And he cast down the pieces of silver in the temple, and departed, and went and hanged himself" (Matt. 27:5).

Evil Thoughts: '"Then did they spit in his face, and buffeted him; and others smote him with the palms of their hands"' (Matt. 26:67).

Denial: '"I do not know the man"' (Matt. 26:72).

False Witness: '"Give God the praise: we know that this man is a sinner"' (John 9:24).

Dishonor: '"Crucify him, crucify him"' (Luke 23:21).

Vengeance: 'Nail him to the tree of good and evil. Force him to submit to the serpent!'

Darkness: '"And it was about the sixth hour, and there was a darkness over all the earth until the ninth hour. And the sun was darkened, and the veil of the temple was rent in the midst"' (Luke 23:44–45).

Pathos: '"And he rolled a great stone to the door of the sepulchre, and departed"' (Matt. 27:60).

Dragon: 'Drown out the message!'

Subtle Distraction: 'Put the new wine in the old bottles: wrap the message up in ceremonies and idle repetition.'

Apathy: 'Get them to ignore the OPEN BOOK by making it appear to be too difficult to understand.'

Lust: 'Dilute the truth by making it bland pabulum for the masses, superficial religion; comparatively, material living will appear to be more interesting.'

Hypocrisy: 'Let *me* tell you what love is. I am your lover.'

Intellectual Diversion: 'Flood the market with lengthy discussions of untested hypotheses, historical meanderings, scholastic theology, egocentric religion, and atheistic ethics. Perhaps they will become satisfied with wrong answers.'

Defiance: 'What OPEN BOOK? What Holy Ghost? What Comforter?'

Illegitimacy: 'Discredit the author.'

Intoxicated Ego: 'Get the disciples to gloat over their own successes.'

Division: 'Religion on the brain will give them a variety of sects. They will turn against each other.'

Distraction: 'Keep them enamored with their bodies, their bank accounts, and their precious holy libraries.'

Hypnotism: 'Substitute hypnotic slumber for prayer: "And he cometh unto the disciples, and findeth them asleep, and saith unto Peter, What, could ye not watch with me one hour?"' (Matt. 26:40).

Perversion: 'This is easy. Permit them to do whatever they want, and justify it by saying that since matter has no power and is unknown to God, they can get away with anything. What's the difference? Everybody does it!'

Isolation: 'Keep the ones who know the Comforter separate from each other and their receptive audiences. Cripple their movements by inhumane laws. Refuse to publish their messages.'

Murder: 'Breathe out threats and slaughter against the enlightened ones, but do it subtly so no one suspects deception.'

When we first peck a hole in our shells and the light of Truth pours in, why does the dragon appear within moments of the enlightenment to steal away our joy? It is because we resist identifying with our own prophecy and are doubtful of ever fulfilling it. This is the "war in heaven" (human consciousness) that goes on continually until it becomes so severe that we give up the unclean spirits coming out of the mouth of the dragon. Then all sense of sin and hypocrisy disappears.

15 **Behold, I come as a thief. Blessed is he that watcheth, and keepeth his garments, lest he walk naked, and they see his shame.**

A microbe of hatred, arrogance, or hypocrisy blocks the light of Love. Any excuse is as bad as any other and is inner blindness. The light of Truth, like a blazing sun at noontide, sees through every sin and pretense; it pinpoints our mistakes, enflaming our guilt with blazing intensity. Purity is transparent to divine Love and is the only garment without shame.

16 **And he gathered them together into a place called in the Hebrew tongue Armageddon.**

There is no escape, no putting off for another day. This is the moment that we all dread, the moment when we come face to face with our own wickedness and can no longer hide. We stand before Judge Truth and know that we are guilty as hell.

17 **And the seventh angel poured out his vial into the air; and there came a great voice out of the temple of heaven, from the throne, saying, It is done.**

Seventh Vial: 'Here is the miracle of Love. Judge Truth cannot see any evil in you. Divine Love radiates, "Behold my son, he is perfect."'

18 **And there were voices, and thunders, and lightnings; and there was a great earthquake, such as was not since men were upon the earth, so mighty an earthquake, and so great.**

The mind retraces all of life's frail experiences in a moment of time. Nothing that the angel said coincides with our experience. We are dumbfounded!

Shock of Disbelief: 'It does not make any sense. How can every thought without God be false? Yes, I am guilty, but how can my whole life be a mistake?'

19 **And the great city was divided into three parts, and the cities of the nations fell: and great Babylon came in remembrance before God, to give unto her the cup of the wine of the fierceness of his wrath.**

Seventh Vial: 'Life, Truth, and Love have always been One. You were taught this identity as Father, Son, and Holy Ghost.'

Crumbling Man—666: 'Three times and in three ways I have failed: I tried to have a life of my own; I thought I was separate from God—unworthy to be called a son; and I was fooled by mental and animal subtlety into thinking that Christ was a mystery—convinced that the divine pneuma, the OPEN BOOK, the Comforter, or the Holy Ghost was completely unbelievable and, therefore, should be ignored, belittled, or destroyed.

'The only possible conclusion is that there is no life in matter, no truth in mortal man's mind, and no Love of this world. Everything that I have thought is being ripped from my grasp.'

20 **And every island fled away, and the mountains were not found.**

As egotism loses its foothold on man, personal isolation and mountainous tribulations disappear. We are getting ready to witness the *sea of glass*.

21 **And there fell upon men a great hail out of heaven, every stone about the weight of a talent: and men blasphemed God because of the plague of the hail; for the plague thereof was exceeding great.**

The Last Stand: 'My guilt of believing in a lie is more than I can stand. I feel like a monster. How can you say there is no evil in me? How can you say that I am your son? I don't deserve to be loved. There is nothing left of me! I am finished.'

And when I saw him, I fell at his feet as dead (Rev. 1:17).

Vision 5

JUDGMENT OF THE GREAT WHORE

Rev. 17

1 And there came one of the seven angels which had the
seven vials, and talked with me, saying unto me, "Come
hither; I will shew unto thee

THE JUDGMENT OF THE GREAT WHORE

that sitteth upon many waters:

2 With whom the kings of the earth have committed
fornication, and the inhabitants of the earth have been made
drunk with the wine of her fornication."

3 So he carried me away in the spirit into the wilderness: and
I saw a woman sit upon
a scarlet coloured beast, full of names of blasphemy,
having

SEVEN HEADS and TEN HORNS.

4 And the woman was arrayed in purple and scarlet colour,
and decked with gold and precious stones and pearls,
having a golden cup in her hand full of abominations and
filthiness of her fornication:
5 And upon her forehead was a name written,

MYSTERY,
BABYLON THE GREAT,
THE MOTHER OF HARLOTS AND ABOMINATIONS
OF THE EARTH.

6 And I saw the woman drunken with the blood of the saints,
and with the blood of the martyrs of Jesus: and when I saw
her, I wondered with great admiration.
7 And the angel said unto me, "Wherefore didst thou marvel?
I will tell thee the mystery of the woman, and of the beast
that carrieth her, which hath the seven heads and ten horns.
8 The beast that thou sawest was, and is not; and shall ascend
out of the bottomless pit, and go into perdition: and they
that dwell on the earth shall wonder, whose names were not

written in the book of life from the foundation of the world,
when they behold the beast that was, and is not, and yet is."

9 And **here is the mind that hath wisdom**.
• The seven heads are seven mountains, on which the
woman sitteth.

10 • And there are seven kings: five are fallen, and one is, and
the other is not yet come; and when he cometh, he must
continue a short space.

11 • And the beast that was, and is not, even he is the eighth,
and is of the seven, and goeth into perdition.

12 • And the ten horns which thou sawest are ten kings, which
have received no kingdom as yet; but receive power as
kings one hour with the beast.
13 These have one mind, and shall give their power and
strength unto the beast.
14 These shall make war with the Lamb, and the Lamb shall
overcome them: for he is Lord of lords, and King of kings:
and they that are with him are called, and chosen, and
faithful.

15 And he saith unto me,
• "The waters which thou sawest, where the whore sitteth,
are peoples, and multitudes, and nations, and tongues."

16 • "And the ten horns which thou sawest upon the beast,
these shall hate the whore, and shall make her desolate and
naked, and shall eat her flesh, and burn her with fire.

17 For God hath put in their hearts to fulfil his will, and to
agree, and give their kingdom unto the beast, until the
words of God shall be fulfilled."

18 • "And the woman which thou sawest is that great city,
which reigneth over the kings of the earth."

Judgment of The Great Whore

The Offense of Lust

Rev. 17

In the previous two chapters, everything that we held dear unto ourselves as mortals—the physical senses and all the paraphernalia of the human mind—was under attack from the advancing spiritual testimony. What is so precious that we would deny God in order to retain it? What secret indulgence is so important to us that we would crucify both the messenger and the message of Truth and Love rather than dispense with it? What is it that we are willing to die for? It is the great whore of our own lustful imagination.

> Every man is tempted, when he is drawn away of his own lust, and enticed. Then when lust hath conceived, it bringeth forth sin: and sin, when it is finished, bringeth forth death (James 1:14–15).

The Comforter will not leave us dreaming in the wilderness forever. Like a sculptor beholding a perfect model, Christ chips away at our foibles until the likeness of God appears. But we, clinging to a mass of desires, resist the blessed chisel that the angels with the plagues present. To help loosen our grip, one of the angel testifiers reappears to show us the incriminating evidence: an animated, color-enhanced exposé of our secret passions. Lust must be seen for what it is and for what it is not before we are willing to let it go.

1–2 **And there came one of the seven angels which had the seven vials, and talked with me, saying unto me, Come hither; I will shew unto thee the judgment of the great whore that sitteth upon many waters: With whom the kings of the earth have committed fornication, and the inhabitants of the earth have been made drunk with the wine of her fornication.**

One of the messengers, or all the evidence condensed into a form that could be understood as one, enabled John to see the incredible contrivance of the human mind and how it is to be judged. The First Commandment, "Thou shalt have no other gods before me" (Exod. 20:3), warns against this contrivance, but we find the attraction irresistible. Heedless of the dreadful consequences, we feed our vivid imaginations with a sense of lustful adventure and defend our right to have it with dizzying intensity.

3 **So he carried me away in the spirit into the wilderness: and I saw a woman sit upon a scarlet coloured beast, full of names of blasphemy, having seven heads and ten horns.**

Having witnessed the rebellion of the human mind and body against its own enlightenment, John was carried back into the mental wilderness where the human mind pursues its own passions. Here he saw sensuous man, full of lust and hypocrisy, carrying on his back his burden of choice: his own imagination, figured as a woman—the antithesis of the Woman clothed with the sun in chapter 12. This man is decked in the full regalia of self-importance and self-indulgence, knowing full well the Mosaic Decalogue but choosing to deny it.

It is interesting to note that John had no such burden. The angel was freely carrying him in Spirit, whereas sensuous man could not be lifted up.

4 **And the woman was arrayed in purple and scarlet colour, and decked with gold and precious stones and pearls, having a golden cup in her hand full of abominations and filthiness of her fornication:**

The woman was wrapped in elegant duplicity: self-confident ego on the one hand and the seduction of licentious corruption on the other, both enticing us at every opportunity to gloat over our own charade. The precious stones that should be fastened to the breastplate of righteousness are, instead, costume jewelry flaunted as a veil of pretence. Rather than the singular pearls of wisdom in the open gates of the holy city, we see many vain platitudes adorning the neck with lies.

The golden cup that is held by the woman is not genuine gold because the container that feeds the imagination is never real. The pictures we entertain in our minds have nothing whatsoever to do with the Mind of God; therefore, all the pictures are distorted. Regardless of whether the view is good or bad, well intentioned or mischievous, it is inaccurate. Since real gold is a symbol of divine Love, *golden* is a symbol of lustful love.

5 **And upon her forehead was a name written, MYSTERY, BABYLON THE GREAT, THE MOTHER OF HARLOTS AND ABOMINATIONS OF THE EARTH.**

This woman is a composite of all the enticements known to man since Eve tasted the forbidden fruit. Adam was the one who broke the Lord's command, and he represents the physical senses. Disobedient man plants the thorns along the path and is a persecutor of prophets and apostles. The MOTHER OF HARLOTS represents the motivation behind sinful acts and, therefore, hates the true motivator—divine Love. Adam and the physical senses deny Christ, Truth. This symbolic woman is that which mocks any awareness of divine Love.

The headlines of all earth's stories are fabulous productions based on the theme of Adam and Eve: disobedience makes one feel alone, and seduction makes one feel naked. As a result, mankind thinks there is a great problem of being that cannot be solved. To mankind, existence begins as a mystery, grows old with much ado about nothing, and concludes in doom.

The woman's three titles prove her guilt, which divides her asunder in Rev. 16:19: "The great city was divided into three parts"—MYSTERY, BABYLON THE GREAT, and THE MOTHER OF HARLOTS AND ABOMINATIONS OF THE EARTH.

6 **And I saw the woman drunken with the blood of the saints, and with the blood of the martyrs of Jesus: and when I saw her, I wondered with great admiration.**

Even John was momentarily engrossed by the horrible fantasy illustrating the power of the imagination whereby every earth-based thought is an inebriate found persecuting Christ's message and messengers. Jesus' blood is not mentioned here because he never carried the burden of lust.

7–8 **And the angel said unto me, Wherefore didst thou marvel? I will tell thee the mystery of the woman, and of the beast that carrieth her, which hath the seven heads and ten horns. The beast that thou sawest was, and is not; and shall ascend out of the bottomless pit, and go into perdition: and they that dwell on the earth shall wonder, whose names were not written in the book of life from the foundation of the world, when they behold the beast that was, and is not, and yet is.**

No aspect of matter ever lives, but the truth of this statement is inexplicable to the woman or to mortal man. Every picture in a dream is within the mind of the dreamer alone and is not a product of Mind (God). The dreamer unconsciously blocks awareness of his true identity because he is preoccupied with his own enticements.

Fortunately, under the scrutiny of Christ, everything returns to it roots. The illusion that finite life can attach itself to matter, motivate itself by lust, and call itself man is the beast that was, and is not. Christ and the Comforter educate mortals out of this illusion, yet for them it is an inexplicable wonder.

> And they were astonished out of measure, saying among themselves, Who then can be saved? And Jesus looking upon them saith, With men it is impossible, but not with God: for with God all things are possible (Mark 10:26–27).

In full realization of spiritual life, mortality disappears, and man is seen as the image and likeness of God. In spite of ourselves and our false beliefs, man *is*.

9 **And here is the mind which hath wisdom. The seven heads are seven mountains, on which the woman sitteth.**

In Scripture, the prophets regularly sought higher ground to hear the Word. The mountains represent a potential lifting up, which is suppressed when we entertain lust, preventing us from finding the path and ascending above earth-based living. Knowledge of salvation—the seven spirits of God understood—remains under cover until the motivation to sin is overcome. It is as if self-justified man winks at the Comforter and says, 'I know you represent a goldmine of wisdom, but I just don't want to do the work to uncover it.'

10 **And there are seven kings: five are fallen, and one is, and the other is not yet come; and when he cometh, he must continue a short space.**

After the seventh vial was cast into the air, a great voice came out of the temple from the throne, saying, "It is done," and mortal man's beliefs about being a physical entity were finished. The five physical senses have fallen off their makeshift thrones, and lust and hypocrisy—the great whore and Babylon the great—are center stage. The king that "is not yet come; and when he cometh, he must continue a short space" is the idea form (body) of millennial consciousness, discussed later in chapter 20.

11 **And the beast that was, and is not, even he is the eighth, and is of the seven, and goeth into perdition.**

"The last enemy that shall be destroyed is death" (1 Cor. 15:26), and hell follows with him. Perdition is another name for the bottomless pit where death is chained for a season.

12 **And the ten horns which thou sawest are ten kings, which have received no kingdom as yet; but receive power as kings one hour with the beast.**

The Ten Commandments may appear dormant in the minds of men, and man may commit fresh atrocities in total defiance of them, but in this epoch, The Commandments are written within men's foreheads. One by one, they must be brought into conscious realization and the power therein demonstrated.

13–14 **These have one mind, and shall give their power and strength unto the beast. These shall make war with the Lamb, and the Lamb shall overcome them: for he is Lord of lords, and King of kings: and they that are with him are called, and chosen, and faithful.**

Always a liar, the great whore claims that the ten horns make the Ten Commandments optional. A statement of Principle, or law, is Truth expressed. Evil, having no basis in fact, attempts to belittle Principle by suggesting that Truth is merely a hypothesis. As if in a court of law, evil opens its arguments with questions: 'What if we are each our own being, and God has nothing to do with it? What if there is good and bad? What if there is love and lust?'

To the Lamb, the solution is simple and potent: there is no court because there is nothing to judge—no questions, no options, and no considerations. Love has no contests. Man, freed from a mind contrary to good, is a living witness of the true meaning and power of the ten horns.

15 **And he saith unto me, The waters which thou sawest, where the whore sitteth, are peoples, and multitudes, and nations, and tongues.**

All those who indulge in this world carry the burden of lust.

16 **And the ten horns which thou sawest upon the beast, these shall hate the whore, and shall make her desolate and naked, and shall eat her flesh, and burn her with fire.**

When the Ten Commandments are understood and cherished, they will empower man to lift off the burden of lust. MYSTERY, BABYLON THE GREAT, and THE MOTHER OF HARLOTS AND ABOMINATIONS OF THE EARTH will burn like chaff.

17 **For God hath put in their hearts to fulfil his will, and to agree, and give their kingdom unto the beast, until the words of God shall be fulfilled.**

Enlightened humanity will find itself free of all false desires, patiently awaiting the fulfillment of all prophecy.

18 **And the woman which thou sawest is that great city, which reigneth over the kings of the earth.**

Lust is the city of conscious and unconscious suggestions that reigns over a mortal's mind.

Revelation 18

BABYLON IS FALLEN

Rev. 18

1 And after these things I saw another angel come down from
heaven, having great power; and the earth was lightened
with his glory.

2 And he cried mightily with a strong voice, saying,

"BABYLON THE GREAT IS FALLEN,
IS FALLEN,"

and is become the habitation of devils, and the hold of
every foul spirit, and a cage of every unclean and hateful
bird.

3 For all nations have drunk of the wine of the wrath of her
fornication, and the kings of the earth have committed
fornication with her, and the merchants of the earth are
waxed rich through the abundance of her delicacies.

4 And I heard another voice from heaven, saying,
**"Come out of her, my people, that ye be not partakers
of her sins, and that ye receive not of her plagues.**

5 For her sins have reached unto heaven, and God hath
remembered her iniquities.

6 Reward her even as she rewarded you, and double unto her
double according to her works: in the cup which she hath
filled fill to her double.

7 How much she hath glorified herself, and lived deliciously,
so much torment and sorrow give her: for she saith in her
heart,

**'I sit a queen, and am no widow,
and shall see no sorrow.'**

8 Therefore shall her plagues come in one day, death, and
mourning, and famine; and she shall be utterly burned with
fire: for strong is the Lord God who judgeth her.

9 And the kings of the earth, who have committed fornication
and lived deliciously with her, shall bewail her, and lament
for her, when they shall see the smoke of her burning,

10 Standing afar off for the fear of her torment, saying,
'Alas, alas that great city Babylon, that mighty city! for in one hour is thy judgment come.'"

11 "And the merchants of the earth shall weep and mourn over her; for
no man buyeth their merchandise any more:
12 The merchandise of gold, and silver, and precious stones, and of pearls, and fine linen, and purple, and silk, and scarlet, and all thyine wood, and all manner vessels of ivory, and all manner vessels of most precious wood, and of brass, and iron, and marble,
13 And cinnamon, and odours, and ointments, and frankincense, and wine, and oil, and fine flour, and wheat, and beasts, and sheep, and horses, and chariots, and slaves, and souls of men."

14 "And **the fruits that thy soul lusted after are departed from thee,** and all things which were dainty and goodly are departed from thee, and thou shalt find them no more at all.
15 The merchants of these things, which were made rich by her, shall stand afar off for the fear of her torment, weeping and wailing,
16 And saying,
'Alas, alas, that great city, that was clothed in fine linen, and purple, and scarlet, and decked with gold, and precious stones, and pearls!
17 **For in one hour so great riches is come to nought.'"**

And every shipmaster, and all the company in ships, and sailors, and as many as trade by sea, stood afar off,
18 And cried when they saw the smoke of her burning, saying, "What city is like unto this great city!"
19 And they cast dust on their heads, and cried, weeping and wailing, saying, "Alas, alas, that great city, wherein were made rich all that had ships in the sea by reason of her costliness!" for in one hour is she made desolate.

20 **Rejoice over her, thou heaven, and ye holy apostles and prophets; for God hath avenged you on her.**

21 And a mighty angel took up a stone like a great millstone, and cast it into the sea, saying,
Thus with violence shall that great city Babylon be thrown down, and shall be found no more at all.

22 And the voice of harpers, and musicians, and of pipers, and trumpeters, shall be heard no more at all in thee; and no craftsman, of whatsoever craft he be, shall be found any more in thee; and the sound of a millstone shall be heard no more at all in thee;
23 And the light of a candle shall shine no more at all in thee; And the voice of the bridegroom and of the bride shall be heard no more at all in thee: for thy merchants were the great men of the earth; for by thy sorceries were all nations deceived.

24 **And in her was found the blood of prophets, and of saints, and of all that were slain upon the earth.**

Babylon is Fallen
Downfall of Hypocrisy

Rev. 18
From the first faint prophetic insights to the presentation of the Comforter, we have waited for this day of reckoning: "For dust thou art, and unto dust shalt thou return" (Gen. 3:19). That which we were told would happen—that which we suspected all along—is coming to pass, complete with prophetic news highlights of the events of that fateful day. We have witnessed the folly of subscribing to the theory of a two-power universe and have bowed to Satan's demands for the last time. The composite of good and evil is dead, and we are hurt, disappointed, terrified, and relieved. "Wherefore henceforth know we no man after the flesh" (2 Cor. 5:16). Blessings rarely come in the form that we personally desire because our vision is too distorted to wish correctly; however, they are blessings nonetheless.

Divine Love will not leave us comfortless. As the old bottles containing our fondest convictions are emptied and disposed of, the new dispensation—the truth of being—is present to fill the void and define the outline of the Son of man.

> Though we have known Christ after the flesh, yet now henceforth know we him no more. Therefore if any man be in Christ, he is a new creature: old things are passed away; behold, all things are become new (2 Cor. 5:16–17).

Babylon is neither the physical senses nor lust. These have already been set aside. Babylon the great is hypocrisy. As we become disgusted with the lustful impulses of the great whore and move away from them, the suggestion fades away.

The culprit was always lust and hypocrisy, otherwise known as mortal mind. It was the so-called intelligence of mortal mind that produced all the effect of the five physical senses in the first place. Now the fact that mortal mind must also fall is coming to pass, making way for the truth of being to be realized. The old things must pass away—Babylon the great is fallen. Rejoice!

1 **And after these things I saw another angel come down from heaven, having great power; and the earth was lightened with his glory.**

John could see that as the heaven-sent truth of Christ's message begins to dawn on us, earth's shadows fade, preparing us for a new and brighter view of reality as spiritual substance. He that hath eyes to see is beginning to see with God's eyes.

2 **And he cried mightily with a strong voice, saying, Babylon the great is fallen, is fallen, and is become the habitation of devils, and the hold of every foul spirit, and a cage of every unclean and hateful bird.**

Reverberating throughout our mental cell, we hear the dreaded fate of our own imagined life: the mistake of mortal mentality resounds in our spiritual ears. Devils or evils had so sickened our mental potential that we flew off to scavenge for things of this world, like vultures for carrion.

> As a cage is full of birds, so are their houses full of deceit: therefore they are become great, and waxen rich (Jer. 5:27).

3 **For all nations have drunk of the wine of the wrath of her fornication, and the kings of the earth have committed fornication with her, and the merchants of the earth are waxed rich through the abundance of her delicacies.**

Entranced by gluttony, sitting on our self-fabricated mental thrones, hypocrisy abounds with many gods. Our precious possessions have been worth more to us than spiritual riches.

> Jesus beholding him loved him, and said unto him, One thing thou lackest: go thy way, sell whatsoever thou hast, and give to the poor, and thou shalt have treasure in heaven: and come, take up the cross, and follow me. And he was sad at that saying, and went away grieved: for he had great possessions (Mark 10:21–22).

4–5 **And I heard another voice from heaven, saying, Come out of her, my people, that ye be not partakers of her sins, and that ye receive not of her plagues. For her sins have reached unto heaven, and God hath remembered her iniquities.**

Sin is exposed and knows it. Since the all-knowing Mind knows only good, the motivator of sin is striped of all imagined credibility. We are now fully aware that we have created our own hell and hear the call to come out from the confines of self-propagating thought. We must prove for ourselves that we understand spiritual substance, generated by Mind alone. Conscience and guilt are now working together to break the bonds of hypocrisy.

> Thus saith the Lord God; Behold, O my people, I will open your graves, and cause you to come up out of your graves, and bring you into the land of Israel (Ezek. 37:12).

6 **Reward her even as she rewarded you, and double unto her double according to her works: in the cup which she hath filled fill to her double.**

It is twice as hard to undo an evil than it is to have never partaken of it in the first place. Both the lustful desire and the hypocrisy that animates the sinful act must cease. Mosaic law said that a person convicted of thievery must pay back double restitution for this very reason. Driven by Satan, sinful man acts like a thief attempting to usurp divine authority. Re-establishment of our true identity and restoration of our divine connection require payback—just compensation for pardoned sins.

Speak ye comfortably to Jerusalem, and cry unto her, that her warfare is accomplished, that her iniquity is pardoned: for she hath received of the Lord's hand double for all her sins (Isa 40:2).

7 **How much she hath glorified herself, and lived deliciously, so much torment and sorrow give her: for she saith in her heart, I sit a queen, and am no widow, and shall see no sorrow.**

Blind ambition, full of boastful pretence, sits unrepentant. The liar of all lies promises perpetual pleasure from sin. By the great whore's own declaration, she cannot fulfill Isaiah's prophecy of the Woman.

Fear not; for thou shalt not be ashamed: neither be thou confounded; for thou shalt not be put to shame: for thou shalt forget the shame of thy youth, and shalt not remember the reproach of thy widowhood any more (Isa. 54:4).

8 **Therefore shall her plagues come in one day, death, and mourning, and famine; and she shall be utterly burned with fire: for strong is the Lord God who judgeth her.**

Truth carries the evidence of a clean mind, and Love, a clean heart. Any thought unlike Truth and Love will stand out in violation of conscience. Evil suggestion must first admit its own folly; then, it will suffer in sorrow, witness its own destruction, and die away in the distance.

For our God is a consuming fire (Heb. 12:29).

9–10 **And the kings of the earth, who have committed fornication and lived deliciously with her, shall bewail her, and lament for her, when they shall see the smoke of her burning, Standing afar off for the fear of her torment, saying, Alas, alas that great city Babylon, that mighty city! for in one hour is thy judgment come.**

Knowing in our hearts that we should not think self-generated thoughts does not mean that we will stop thinking them. We are not willing to let *our* thoughts go until an irresistible force in us begins to hate the dream that we behold as earthly consciousness. When this hour arrives, evil becomes nonsense. Awakening from the dream of mortal mind, we see Satan's cause and intent, identify the error, and condemn ourselves as fools for having ever accepted the lie. We first give up the thoughts we hate and then the ones we cherish, but we do not easily surrender the thoughts that give us pleasure. We lament our losses until the transition is complete—until we forget the dream.

> Though thou exalt thyself as the eagle, and though thou set thy nest among the stars, thence will I bring thee down, saith the Lord (Obad. 1:4).

11–14 **And the merchants of the earth shall weep and mourn over her; for no man buyeth their merchandise any more: The merchandise of gold, and silver, and precious stones, and of pearls, and fine linen, and purple, and silk, and scarlet, and all thyine wood, and all manner vessels of ivory, and all manner vessels of most precious wood, and of brass, and iron, and marble, And cinnamon, and odours, and ointments, and frankincense, and wine, and oil, and fine flour, and wheat, and beasts, and sheep, and horses, and chariots, and slaves, and souls of men. And the fruits that thy soul lusted after are departed from thee, and all things which were dainty and goodly are departed from thee, and thou shalt find them no more at all.**

In this context, the gold, pearls, chariots, and other possessions are not material things but are the mental feeling and attitude one has when one desires such things. The delicious juice of the mind that was produced for one's pleasure must now be left behind because God did not think these thoughts.

> Son of man, hast thou seen what the ancients of the house of Israel do in the dark, every man in the chambers of his imagery? (Ezek. 8:12).

Because Jesus knew how to love divinely, those who stood in his way did not prevent him from being lifted up. His comment, "Foxes have holes, and birds of the air have nests; but the Son of man hath not where to lay his head" (Luke 9:58), indicates his total lack of desire for earthly possessions. He was not confined within the shell of mortal mind and, therefore, had no lust in his heart and no attitude in his thought. Leaning on the substance of divine grace alone, Jesus chose not to buy the thoughts of this world.

If one has gained spiritual dominion over mental attitudes, he may use symbols to present that wisdom to his friends as John is doing here, but he who understands ideas spiritually no longer requires symbols. Like a friendship that has been outgrown, the mental posture and its object must be dispensed with in order to ascend. We must comply with the pattern shown to us by the Master.

15–16 **The merchants of these things, which were made rich by her, shall stand afar off for the fear of her torment, weeping and wailing, And saying, Alas, alas, that great city, that was clothed in fine linen, and purple, and scarlet, and decked with gold, and precious stones, and pearls!**

17… **For in one hour so great riches is come to nought.**

Lust is the intoxicant that makes every thought an addiction, and hypocrisy weeps and wails at one's failure to comply with whatever electrifies the mind. The instant Christ breaks one's mental barriers, the intrigue of mortal mind is gone. In the presence of divine Love, there is no trace of lust or hypocrisy, no acknowledgement of it, and no requirement for a period of recovery.

...17 **And every shipmaster, and all the company in ships, and sailors, and as many as trade by sea, stood afar off,**
18–19 **And cried when they saw the smoke of her burning, saying, What city is like unto this great city! And they cast dust on their heads, and cried, weeping and wailing, saying, Alas, alas, that great city, wherein were made rich all that had ships in the sea by reason of her costliness! for in one hour is she made desolate.**

Hypocrisy is the purveyor of lust. Floating on the sea of error, the false prophet knows he is doomed, for in the presence of Mind, there is no longer anything to convey.

> My God hath sent his angel, and hath shut the lions' mouths (Dan. 6:22).

When the Comforter arrives, the man made of dust fails to please, fails to deliver, and fails to survive divine scrutiny. Every element on the swollen sea of error is on fire. Mortal mind, the dust magnet that was written in our foreheads, is returned to its source—nothingness.

> If a man abide not in me, he is cast forth as a branch, and is withered; and men gather them, and cast them into the fire, and they are burned (John 15:6).

20 **Rejoice over her, thou heaven, and ye holy apostles and prophets; for God hath avenged you on her.**

This drama is presented for our benefit as an object lesson to help sever the relationship between the human mind and error and to prepare the way for the Son of man. Christ demands recognition of the spiritual source and gratitude for the bitter experience before we can be lifted up.

> And Jesus lifted up his eyes, and said, Father, I thank thee that thou hast heard me (John 11:41).

21 **And a mighty angel took up a stone like a great millstone, and cast it into the sea, saying, Thus with violence shall that great city Babylon be thrown down, and shall be found no more at all.**

Truth pummels the lie; Love dissolves the liar. The sea of error will receive its deathblow and be ground to powder, never to reappear. Lust and hypocrisy shall be known "no more at all."

22–23 **And the voice of harpers, and musicians, and of pipers, and trumpeters, shall be heard no more at all in thee; and no craftsman, of whatsoever craft he be, shall be found any more in thee; and the sound of a millstone shall be heard no more at all in thee; And the light of a candle shall shine no more at all in thee; and the voice of the bridegroom and of the bride shall be heard no more at all in thee: for thy merchants were the great men of the earth; for by thy sorceries were all nations deceived.**

All activity that was once thought to be desirable and necessary for the fulfillment of happiness is set aside, for now it is understood that happiness resides in spiritual presence without those things. The apparatus that once mimicked divine activity has been replaced by the divine activity.

> The children of this world marry, and are given in marriage: But they which shall be accounted worthy to obtain that world, and the resurrection from the dead, neither marry, nor are given in marriage (Luke 20:34–35).

24 **And in her was found the blood of prophets, and of saints, and of all that were slain upon the earth.**

Mortal mind animates the persecutors of the saints and prophets and is the oppressor of the earth, distracting mankind away from the true light. None of this drama called human history would have been possible without the supposition of a power opposed to God.

> He therefore that despiseth, despiseth not man, but God, who hath also given unto us his holy Spirit (I Thess. 4:8).

Revelation 19

ALLELUIA
and an Invitation to
The Marriage of the Lamb

Rev. 19

1 And after these things I heard a great voice of much people
in heaven, saying,

"Alleluia; Salvation, and glory, and honour, and power,
2 **unto the Lord our God: for true and righteous are his**
judgments: for he hath judged the great whore, which
did corrupt the earth with her fornication, and hath
avenged the blood of his servants at her hand."

3 And again they said, **"Alleluia."**

And her smoke rose up for ever and ever.

4 And the four and twenty elders and the four beasts fell
down and worshipped God that sat on the throne, saying,
"Amen; Alleluia."

5 And a voice came out of the throne, saying, Praise our God,
all ye his servants, and ye that fear him, both small and
great.
6 And I heard as it were the voice of a great multitude, and as
the voice of many waters, and as the voice of mighty
thunderings, saying,

"Alleluia: for the Lord God omnipotent reigneth.
7 **Let us be glad and rejoice, and give Honour to him: for**

THE MARRIAGE OF THE LAMB IS COME,

and

his wife hath made herself ready."

8 And to her was granted that she should be arrayed in fine
linen, clean and white: for the fine linen is the
righteousness of saints.

9 And he saith unto me, Write,
"Blessed are they which are called unto the marriage supper of the Lamb."

And he saith unto me, "These are the true sayings of God."

10 And I fell at his feet to worship him.
And he said unto me, "See thou do it not: I am thy fellowservant, and of thy brethren that have the testimony of Jesus:

worship God:

for the testimony of Jesus is the spirit of prophecy."

11 And I saw heaven opened, and behold a WHITE HORSE;
and he that sat upon him was
called FAITHFUL and TRUE,
and in righteousness he doth judge and make war.
12 • His **eyes were as a flame of fire**,
• and **on his head were many crowns**;
• and **he had a name written, that no man knew, but he himself.**
13 • And he was clothed with **a vesture dipped in blood:**
• and his name is called THE WORD OF GOD.

14 And the armies which were in heaven followed him upon
white horses, clothed in fine linen, white and clean.

15 And out of his mouth goeth a sharp sword, that with it
• he should smite the nations: and
• he shall rule them with a rod of iron: and
• he treadeth the winepress of the fierceness and wrath of Almighty God.

16 And he hath on his vesture and on his thigh a name written,
KING OF KINGS, AND LORD OF LORDS.

17 **And I saw an angel standing in the sun;**
and he cried with a loud voice, saying to all the fowls that fly in the midst of heaven,

"Come and gather yourselves together
unto the supper of the great God;

18 That ye may eat the flesh of kings, and the flesh of captains, and the flesh of mighty men, and the flesh of horses, and of them that sit on them, and the flesh of all men, both free and bond, both small and great."

19 And I saw the beast, and the kings of the earth, and their armies, gathered together to make war against him that sat on the horse, and against his army.

20 And the BEAST was taken, and with him the FALSE PROPHET THAT WROUGHT MIRACLES before him, with which he deceived them that had received the mark of the beast, and them that worshipped his image.

These both were cast alive into a lake of fire burning with brimstone.

21 **And the remnant were slain with the sword of him that sat upon the horse, which sword proceeded out of his mouth: and all the fowls were filled with their flesh.**

ALLELUIA
and an Invitation to The Marriage of the Lamb

Rev. 19

Chapters 15 through18 (the casting of the seven vials, the great whore, and the fall of Babylon) illustrate mortal man's warfare with himself as Christ presents the facts of being to him. Ultimately, Truth and Love save man from himself, lifting him out of his suicidal mental breakdown.

Now the grand triumph of Truth and Love is heralded from above (within resurrection consciousness). The dramatic scenes in the previous chapters do not trouble those who know the truth and have already gained their inheritance, for they already know the end from the beginning.

When men crucified the flesh of Jesus, they witnessed his bitter experience, his death, and his wrapped body in a tomb. Then a great stone was rolled over the doorway of the sepulcher, and the men departed. Humanly, Jesus was left alone in a cave, but he was, actually, attended to by a multitude of angels and omnipresent Life. The tomb became his laboratory where he would work out the simple solution to the great problem of being.

What do you suppose Jesus was conscious of while he lay reposed on a stone? If he were aware of this world's senses, he would have been feeling intense pain. If he were thinking about all the disciples who had run away in fear, he would have been disappointed. If he were reflecting on his life experience, he would have been tempted to be nostalgic. If he had been conscious of anything of this world or if he were dead, he would have stayed in the grave and shortly returned to dust like a mortal. But if Jesus' statements are true, would it not be safe to say that they were still in effect right there in the tomb? Consider the relevance of the eighth Beatitude to the moment at hand.

> Blessed are they which are persecuted for righteousness' sake: for theirs is the kingdom of heaven (Matt. 5:10).

The term *blessed* could be more accurately translated as *walk forth with joy*. Is not that precisely what Jesus was doing—living his own Beatitude and walking forth in the kingdom of heaven? Now for the first time in Scripture, we are invited to witness the mental altitude exemplified by the Master, which enabled him to raise himself from the dead and announce the divine pattern of ascension to every listening ear.

We are about to witness the true power and just rewards of gratitude: entertaining angels on a grand scale in an alleluia chorus and preparations for the marriage of the Lamb and the Lamb's wife. For Jesus and all men, a glorious day was dawning inside the tomb, and it took every ounce of that grand preparation to roll away the stone and reveal the bridegroom.

For most of us, our trial is not quite so dramatic, but the pattern has been set. No part will be left out of our own proof of God's love, and the requirement for gratitude is no less stringent. When we do our own work faithfully, as Jesus did, and walk forth with joy, we will be ready to partake of the marriage feast. Here is our invitation to witness the birth of the child caught up unto God and to His throne.

1–2 **And after these things I heard a great voice of much people in heaven, saying, Alleluia; Salvation, and glory, and honour, and power, unto the Lord our God: For true and righteous are his judgments: for he hath judged the great whore, which did corrupt the earth with her fornication, and hath avenged the blood of his servants at her hand.**

Gratitude for Christ resounds throughout the opened chambers of thought, enabling the listener to hear the grand chorus of Truth where the mind made deaf by lust used to be. When one acknowledges completely the *source* as all good, there is nothing left to judge.

3 **And again they said, Alleluia. And her smoke rose up for ever and ever.**

Having no thoughts of self, spiritualized man echoes creative Mind. A heart filled with joy sings praises continually, for within that heart there is no mist origin capable of entertaining the slightest evil suggestion. Every attempt of lust is burned up without a trace because there is no place for it.

4 **And the four and twenty elders and the four beasts fell down and worshipped God that sat on the throne, saying, Amen; Alleluia.**

Rejoicing in one accord, omnipotence acknowledges no other power, omniscience declares no other law, omnipresence knows no other awareness, and omni-action is moved by no other cause than the one and only Good.

5 **And a voice came out of the throne, saying, Praise our God, all ye his servants, and ye that fear him, both small and great.**

Individually and collectively, every idea of Mind receives the same grand impulse and spontaneously broadcasts the joyful message.

6 **And I heard as it were the voice of a great multitude, and as the voice of many waters, and as the voice of mighty thunderings, saying, Alleluia: for the Lord God omnipotent reigneth.**

The outward expression, motivated by the inner voice, repeats the *I Am* chorus as one resounding presence. There is no other.

7 **Let us be glad and rejoice, and give honour to him: for the marriage of the Lamb is come, and his wife hath made herself ready.**

Rejoice! It is time to prepare for the wedding.

> Touch me not; for I am not yet ascended to my Father: but go to my brethren, and say unto them, I ascend unto my Father, and your Father; and to my God, and your God (John 20:17).

Resurrection consciousness, free of the tomb of material living, is the Lamb; the Woman clothed in light, wearing a crown of twelve stars, prefigures a wife prepared. Her child, soon to be caught up onto God, illustrates the man of God's creating who is about to ascend to the comprehension of Love wedded to its idea.

8 **And to her was granted that she should be arrayed in fine linen, clean and white: for the fine linen is the righteousness of saints.**

As linen has no animal composition, the appearance of the bride expresses no animal characteristics—immaculate Love is arrayed with intelligent innocence. Impurity is null and void.

> The prince of this world cometh, and hath nothing in me (John 14:30).

9 **And he saith unto me, Write, Blessed are they which are called unto the marriage supper of the Lamb. And he saith unto me, These are the true sayings of God.**

A voice from the throne instructed John to address the wedding invitations: "Write, Blessed are they which are called unto the marriage supper of the Lamb." Resurrection consciousness is summoned to come and taste the ascension.

10 **And I fell at his feet to worship him. And he said unto me, See thou do it not: I am thy fellowservant, and of thy brethren that have the testimony of Jesus: worship God: for the testimony of Jesus is the spirit of prophecy.**

Even though John was on the spiritual path, he was tempted to mentally prostrate himself to those spiritually advanced individuals who helped him, as if they were somehow better than he was. John illustrated how precisely we must differentiate between cause and effect. (The First Commandment is the supreme statute regarding worship.) Accepting the invitation to follow Jesus in *the way* is the first step toward understanding the prophecy and fulfillment of man.

11 **And I saw heaven opened, and behold a white horse; and he that sat upon him was called Faithful and True, and in righteousness he doth judge and make war.**

As the sepulcher stone was rolled away, the open doorway revealed the bridegroom, prepared and exalted with the pure power of righteousness. Christ has never failed to present the truth to every waking thought. Since Truth and error cannot exist together, there seems to be a battle line of judgment, but this is only taking place in the minds of mortals and not in the heaven that the Lamb presents to exalted consciousness.

12 **His eyes were as a flame of fire, and on his head were many crowns; and he had a name written, that no man knew, but he himself.**

The all-seeing idea of Mind, presented as Lamb and bridegroom, penetrates through the imagined shadows of the earthly minded, sits down on the throne of God, and wears the crowns that Truth and Love have bestowed. Although Christ consciousness is infinite, universal, and knowable, each individual expression of truth has its own identity. We may share Jesus' thoughts as John did, but no one could take the place of Jesus or claim his identity. Each one of us is the center of God's universe from our individual perspectives.

13 **And he was clothed with a vesture dipped in blood: and his name is called The Word of God.**

He who was first to voluntarily lay himself on the altar was empowered to be the mouthpiece for "every word that proceedeth out of the mouth of God" (Matt. 4:4). The Master took on the burden of the world's sins and wore the cloak of matter to illustrate the way for all men, but he never allowed the doctrine of devils to enter or possess his own thought.

14 **And the armies which were in heaven followed him upon white horses, clothed in fine linen, white and clean.**

The groom's fearless entourage is empowered by the same Truth and clothed by the same Love that the groom manifests. Every idea is arrayed "like unto the Son of man."

15 **And out of his mouth goeth a sharp sword, that with it he should smite the nations: and he shall rule them with a rod of iron: and he treadeth the winepress of the fierceness and wrath of Almighty God.**

All the horror, pain, and disappointment that rebellious mortal man suffers—the seven vials poured out, the great whore, and the falling of Babylon—are instigated by one inescapable voice: omnipotent Truth uttering itself.

16 **And he hath on his vesture and on his thigh a name written, KING OF KINGS, AND LORD OF LORDS.**

The dominion man's outward identity and expression of power and authority, coupled with the intimate promise to exact every element of Truth, rightfully bears the title of KING OF KINGS and LORD OF LORDS, for God and idea coincide as One.

17–18 **And I saw an angel standing in the sun; and he cried with a loud voice, saying to all the fowls that fly in the midst of heaven, Come and gather yourselves together unto the supper of the great God; That ye may eat the flesh of kings, and the flesh of captains, and the flesh of mighty men, and the flesh of horses, and of them that sit on them, and the flesh of all men, both free and bond, both small and great.**

This angel, standing as perfect integrity within the source of divine light and Life, calls out to all pure aspirations that soar above earth's plagues: "Come and gather yourselves together unto the supper of the great God." The call is universal, the feast of Truth and Love is prepared, and the OPEN BOOK is the correct translation of the menu. The feast no longer appears bitter to digest as it was at our first reading because all our objections to its simple explanations have been summarily removed. This food is perfect. The invitation to come and eat of the communion of God and man repeats Jesus' standing offer: "Take, eat; this is my body, [My truth]" (Matt. 26:26).

Regardless of our lot in life, as we do the works and gain mastery over all error in the way Jesus demonstrated, our consciousness becomes palatable to one another and to the *great God,* for we are eating the fruits of Life, Truth, and Love.

19 **And I saw the beast, and the kings of the earth, and their armies, gathered together to make war against him that sat on the horse, and against his army.**

When the pastor of the marriage ceremony asks, 'Is anyone opposed to this marriage?' it is mortal man who stands ready to object. The man of dust, speaking with Satan's mouth, can never understand infinite Truth and Love and, therefore, opposes man's ascension.

20 **And the beast was taken, and with him the false prophet that wrought miracles before him, with which he deceived them that had received the mark of the beast, and them that worshipped his image. These both were cast alive into a lake of fire burning with brimstone.**

Mankind must witness the destruction of evil for himself, or he will never leave it. Christ separates and destroys all false desires and blind justification from the identity of man. Since there is no power apart from God, Christ (the pastor) declares, 'Objection overruled!' and all the evidence of opposition to the marriage is expunged from the record.

21 **And the remnant were slain with the sword of him that sat upon the horse, which sword proceeded out of his mouth: and all the fowls were filled with their flesh.**

Bad habits are hard to break, so truth continues to point out these foolish thought-rituals until every morsel of them is removed. Pain and guilt are the vulture reminders that peck away at the mind of falsehood until every infraction is forgotten.

Vision 7

A THOUSAND YEARS

Rev. 20

1 And I saw an angel come down from heaven, having
the key of the bottomless pit and
a great chain in his hand.
2 And he laid hold on the dragon, that old serpent, which is
the Devil, and Satan, And

bound him

A THOUSAND YEARS,

3 And cast him into the bottomless pit,
and shut him up,
and set a seal upon him,
that he should deceive the nations no more, till the
thousand years should be fulfilled: and after that he must be
loosed a little season.

4 And I saw thrones, and they sat upon them, and judgment
was given unto them: and I saw the souls of them that were
beheaded for the witness of Jesus, and for the word of God,
and which had not worshipped the beast, neither his image,
neither had received his mark upon their foreheads, or in
their hands; and

they lived and reigned with Christ

A THOUSAND YEARS.

5 But the rest of the dead lived not again until the thousand
years were finished.

This is the first resurrection.

6 Blessed and holy is he that hath part in the first
resurrection: on such the second death hath no power, but
they shall be priests of God and of Christ, and shall reign
with him a thousand years.

7 And when the thousand years are expired, Satan shall be
loosed out of his prison,

8 And shall go out to deceive the nations which are in the
four quarters of the earth,

GOG and MAGOG

to gather them together to battle: the number of whom is as
the sand of the sea.

9 And they went up on the breadth of the earth, and
compassed the camp of the saints about, and the beloved
city: and

fire came down from God out of heaven,
and devoured them.

10 And the devil that deceived them was cast into the lake of
fire and brimstone, where the beast and the false prophet
are, and shall be tormented day and night for ever and ever.

11 And I saw a GREAT WHITE THRONE, and him that sat
on it, from whose face the earth and the heaven fled away;
and there was found no place for them.

12 And I saw the dead, small and great, stand before God;

and

THE BOOKS WERE OPENED:

and

another book was opened, which is

THE BOOK OF LIFE:

and the dead were judged out of those things which were
written in the books, according to their works.

13 And the sea gave up the dead which were in it; and death
and hell delivered up the dead which were in them: and
they were judged every man according to their works.

14 **And death and hell were cast into the lake of fire.**

This is the second death.

15 **And whosoever was not found written in the book of life**
was cast into the lake of fire.

A Thousand Years
Resurrected Life

Rev. 20
Early in Jesus' experience, he dismissed the allure of sin and hypocrisy as invalid. Through the tragedy of his crucifixion, he was tempted again, but this time with death and hell. During this trial, he never lost his direct communion with God. The sweet angel chorus, reminding him of divine Life and of all the prophetic promises written about him, assured Jesus that he could not die. He awakened to an enlightened sense of life as resurrection. When Jesus walked forth from the tomb, there was no element of evil capable of reaching his thought or physically touching him. He had entered the state of consciousness in which he had proven for himself, and ultimately for all mankind, that no condition of matter could kill the Son of man. Yet his work was not entirely complete. The *other* king mentioned in Rev. 17:10[*] had to first be embodied and "continue a short space" while its sense of limitation was mastered.

What appeared first to Mary and later to Jesus' disciples was the same man that they had placed in a sepulcher three days earlier, but there was a difference that they had no words to describe. Mary supposed him to be the gardener until she turned to see his true identity. On the walk to Emmaus, two of Jesus' disciples did not even recognize him until the breaking of bread. Seven of his closest apostles, wasting the night fishing on the Sea of Tiberias, knew him not, until Jesus directed them to a massive catch. What was the countenance of this man who appeared to tarry, continuing a short space before his ascension? For Jesus,

---

[*] "And there are seven kings: five are fallen, and one is, and the other is not yet come; and when he cometh, he must continue a short space" (Rev. 17:10).

the millennium had arrived. Resurrection consciousness is millennial consciousness.

The pattern of redemption has been illustrated by Jesus' sublime example, and now it is we who must walk through the states and stages of our own crucifixion and realize millennial joy. Every thought is about to be judged by Christ, Truth, and every sense of limitation will be permanently erased, including death and hell. It is not necessary to physically die, as Jesus did on the cross, in order to share in the resurrection. It is a mental parting of the ways and means of mortal sense that delivers resurrection freedom. Any sense of doubt or fear or lack of love will not share in millennial glory, but be of good cheer "for, behold, I create new heavens and a new earth: and the former shall not be remembered, nor come into mind" (Isa. 65:17).

1 **And I saw an angel come down from heaven, having the key of the bottomless pit and a great chain in his hand.**

Inspiration received from above is never wrong. The understanding that holds the key to life and heaven enables one to detect the secrets of death and hell and find the means to chain those lies. (To detect a counterfeit, one must be thoroughly familiar with the original.)

2–3 **And he laid hold on the dragon, that old serpent, which is the Devil, and Satan, and bound him a thousand years, And cast him into the bottomless pit, and shut him up, and set a seal upon him, that he should deceive the nations no more, till the thousand years should be fulfilled: and after that he must be loosed a little season.**

The big bang *appearance* of energy and matter precludes its inevitable disappearance. For those living under the belief that they are composed of matter and require it, they naturally conclude that death is a part of the cycle of life. Every mortal is convinced of this premise, for to him there is no other possible conclusion. Inspiration from above, however, holds the key that proves the premise false.

Because Jesus never lost contact with his divine origin, he held the key insights that would bind the dragon in his pit. Jesus' resurrection and ascension demonstrated that his material body did not constitute his life.

The bottomless pit—the endless downward spiral of ego, pleasure, death, and hell that mortal man experiences—rightfully belongs to its inventor, and Christ properly places the burden of evil upon itself. Through Christ, Satan is shut up. In this state of consciousness, the words that once animated mortal man have ceased, and man has discovered that he is free to move by every word that proceeds out of the mouth of God. The ignorance and malicious intent that once sealed Scriptural texts have been replaced by spiritual understanding, demonstrating its power to seal the doom of the house divided.

Resurrection consciousness is beyond the reach of material law and visibly demonstrates that God's law supersedes physics; however, resurrection is a waymark for man, a temporary glory in which perfect heaven is seen but not fully realized. When Mary approached Jesus at the tomb, he said, "Touch me not; for I am not yet ascended to my Father" (John 20:17). This probationary stage gives man the opportunity to witness for himself the fixity of divine Life, which binds Satan's curse of eternal damnation.

4 **And I saw thrones, and they sat upon them, and judgment was given unto them: and I saw the souls of them that were beheaded for the witness of Jesus, and for the word of God, and which had not worshipped the beast, neither his image, neither had received his mark upon their foreheads, or in their hands; and they lived and reigned with Christ a thousand years.**

There is evidence that many were waiting to understand what Jesus was the first to demonstrate. When the fifth seal was opened, the souls of them that were slain for the Word of God were instructed to "rest yet for a little season, until their fellowservants also and their brethren, that should be killed as they were, should be fulfilled" (Rev. 6:11). These martyrs did not reappear until after Jesus' resurrection.

> And the graves were opened; and many bodies of the saints which slept arose, And came out of the graves after his resurrection, and went into the holy city, and appeared unto many (Matt. 27:52–53).

The great red dragon that stood waiting to devour the child as soon as it was born had failed, for saintliness is focused on the man of God's creating. The patient waiting of the saints during their mental gestation period bore the expected fruit—the demonstration of life, independent of so-called material laws and conditions.

Each one of us is sovereign unto our own mental throne of thoughts. If those thoughts are ideas that belong solely to God as manifestation, then the mental throne upon which one sits is like the one belonging to the Son of man, as Jesus identified himself. Those who strive for this mastery cling to the truth, wait patiently at the door, and receive their reward—the privilege of witnessing and sharing resurrection consciousness.

5 **But the rest of the dead lived not again until the thousand years were finished. This is the first resurrection.**

Having lust and delusion burned out of us against our will (illustrated in chapters 13–18) is not necessarily something for which we would be immediately grateful. Even though these errors have been proven fruitless and powerless, we may still tend to look in the wrong direction, attending to the effect rather than the cause of truth. We may miss the light gleaming behind the two-edged sword. So it is that we are unprepared to enjoy the grandeur of a sinless life. If we are still haunted to some degree by the mortal view of things, we are down there with those beliefs, chained in the bottomless pit with death and hell in suspended animation.

Jesus did not halt in his progress toward heaven. Mortals alone hesitate when they reach death and, therefore, experience that possibility. Jesus illustrated the way through this morass. According to the alleluia praises recorded in chapter 19, the first corrective action was gratitude. He sang his way out of the tomb. Glorious gratitude for every bitter experience was the key that locked death and hell in the bottomless pit and enabled Jesus to rise above the dreaded blankness of material death.

Do we translate every experience back to spiritual cause, as Jesus did, or do we credit the material experience as having been touched by God? If we do the latter, we are down there in the pit with those beliefs and have not risen to the realization of life outside of matter. Mary Magdalene first saw the risen man, Jesus, at the tomb rather than the Christ that had never died. Later, on the Day of Pentecost, the disciples felt the Christ presence that had never left. To Spirit, life never suffers, dies, and lives again.

6 **Blessed and holy is he that hath part in the first resurrection: on such the second death hath no power, but they shall be priests of God and of Christ, and shall reign with him a thousand years.**

Once an individual has seen for himself that matter cannot kill man, he is strengthened to consider the possibility that the entire concept of death is invalid. The earliest biblical record of creation does not include death.

> And God saw every thing that he had made, and, behold, it was very good (Gen. 1:31).

Jesus was the first man to realize this prophetic scripture, and the demand for universal realization continues until the end of time, when we shall all sit down with him at the marriage feast wearing a wedding garment—the image and likeness of God.

And how long is this resurrection day?

> One day is with the Lord as a thousand years, and a thousand years as one day (2 Pet. 3:8).

7–8 **And when the thousand years are expired, Satan shall be loosed out of his prison, And shall go out to deceive the nations which are in the four quarters of the earth, Gog and Magog, to gather them together to battle: the number of whom is as the sand of the sea.**

Living a sinless life in resurrection consciousness requires no defenses against present enemies because there are none. What, then, is the latent lie chained beneath resurrection consciousness?

When Jesus reappeared from the tomb, he was invincible from the human standpoint. He knew that neither matter nor anything of this world could kill him or make him suffer, but some concept of limitation still lingered; otherwise, he would not have had a visible body at all. Even a sinless, perfectly functioning human body in resurrection consciousness does not fulfill Mind's idea of limitless Life. Jesus' resurrection put death and hell in suspension but did not completely eliminate the possibility of death in some future experience. This is the battle line that resurfaced and the one that Truth must win, in order to make way for the ascension in which our concept of form is lost and Mind's concept of infinite form is gained. Death and hell are eliminated as infinite good is realized!

Gog and Magog are the figurative death and hell actors that resurfaced in order to disrupt millennial glory.

9 **And they went up on the breadth of the earth, and compassed the camp of the saints about, and the beloved city: and fire came down from God out of heaven, and devoured them.**

It was life-filled Euphrates that encompassed the land of Eden and defined its borders. Death and hell now try to style themselves as Euphrates, making one final attempt to offer an alternative to one infinite Life made manifest. But how is it possible for evil to enter millennial thought and attack resurrected man? Suppose that you are living as a dominion man in a replenished earth—where sin, disease, and death are unknown—and there is no harm anywhere. Would you be tempted to stay there forever, hearing God and having all your food and mansions richly provided for you? This encompasses our concept of Eden. But this temptation is satanic. Evil's suggestion might sound something like this: 'Why not stay here in Eden with perfect innocence? Do not taste of the tree of good and evil, and do not touch the tree of Life. I will be an impassable river around you to ensure that you are never cast out again.'

After his resurrection, Jesus' statement, "I am not yet ascended to my Father," indicated his receptivity to further enlightenment. He was not tempted to linger. He knew that to linger would be to accept the finite form of body as a viable option in infinity. Unimpressed by false notions, Jesus waited for God to remove this final argument from his thought. To stay fixed forever in resurrection consciousness would be a strange hell. There must be a fundamental shift from thinking that God is all around us, meeting our needs, to realizing that we are the very living of God's life.

Allegorically, when Satan first appeared in protest against God, he fell from heaven as lightning—as random energy striking out on his own, away from good. Truth, the fire that came down from heaven to devour Satan, burned up all evidence, even lies as plentiful as the sand of the sea. It was not necessary for Truth to know error in order to destroy it. A lie is first inflamed and then disintegrates when the evidence of Truth appears.

> What communion hath light with darkness? (2 Cor. 6:14).

This is evil's third and last attempt to be *like God* instead of being *like the Son of man*. Symbolically, it is the last six in the call of wisdom.

> Let him that hath understanding count the number of the beast: for it is the number of a man; and his number is Six hundred threescore and six (Rev. 13:18).

10 **And the devil that deceived them was cast into the lake of fire and brimstone, where the beast and the false prophet are, and shall be tormented day and night for ever and ever.**

Evil's feeble attempts must always fail, and this failure catalyzes our progress toward the ascension. Every false concept presents its own evidence of falsehood, which by reversal saves us from that evil and proves the presence of Christ. In this light, fire and brimstone protect us from evil's suggestion. Even the sea of glass is mingled with fire, not to harm us but to insure our safety.

Noontide glory is removing the final shadows, and Jesus' prophecy is about to be fulfilled: "The last enemy that shall be destroyed is death" (1 Cor. 15:26).

> The beast that was, and is not, even he is the eighth, and is of the seven, and goeth into perdition (Rev. 17:11).

11 **And I saw a great white throne, and him that sat on it, from whose face the earth and the heaven fled away; and there was found no place for them.**

In the presence of God as the acknowledged seat of all effect, every perception received or transmitted within the human imagination blushes and withdraws. Every memory of mortal mind, which was once thought to be the seat of power in a finite mental universe, vanishes from consciousness.

12 **And I saw the dead, small and great, stand before God; and the books were opened: and another book was opened, which is the book of life: and the dead were judged out of those things which were written in the books, according to their works.**

As we find ourselves standing in the living presence of the Comforter, all prophecy rises to its glorious and instantaneous fulfillment. Finally, we understand—the books are opened! All hypotheses, suppositions, claims, conjectures, and considerations presented to Christ for examination stand before the court of Spirit where they are judged according to their works. In the scale of Spirit, the thoughts of mortals and that which propagates them are naught. Divine Life identifies and verifies one and all.

13 **And the sea gave up the dead which were in it; and death and hell delivered up the dead which were in them: and they were judged every man according to their works.**

When Jesus destroyed the belief in material death for himself, he also released those who had already died, or thought they had died, from that so-called universal belief. He brought divine light into hell, breaking the chains that would have bound us forever outside the presence of God.

14 **And death and hell were cast into the lake of fire. This is the second death.**

As we ascend beyond resurrection consciousness and recognize ourselves as God's image and likeness, concepts of limitation and hell do not exist, and all memory of having once believed in them is erased.

15 **And whosoever was not found written in the book of life was cast into the lake of fire.**

Death and hell are not real, and neither is the lake of fire. Do not be fooled into thinking these concepts are part of God or God's plan. The entire purpose of the discussion of evil is to draw us out of the pain of ignorance and into the radiant light of understanding. If the light of Truth were plunged into the darkness of hell, it would no longer be hell, but heaven; this is the mission of Christ that has been, is being, and will be accomplished.

> Thy kingdom come. Thy will be done in earth, as it is in heaven (Matt 6:10).

Vision 7

A NEW HEAVEN AND A NEW EARTH

Rev. 21–22:2

Rev. 21

1 And I saw

A NEW HEAVEN AND A NEW EARTH:

for the first heaven and the first earth were passed away;
and there was

NO MORE SEA.

2 And I John saw

the holy city,

NEW JERUSALEM,

coming down from God out of heaven,

prepared as a bride adorned for her husband.

3 And I heard a great voice out of heaven saying,
"Behold,
- the tabernacle of God is with men, and
- he will dwell with them, and
- they shall be his people, and
- God himself shall be with them, and be their God.

4 And
- God shall wipe away all tears from their eyes; and
- there shall be no more death, neither sorrow, nor crying, neither shall there be any more pain: for
- the former things are passed away."

5 And he that sat upon the throne said,

"Behold, I make all things new."

And he said unto me, "Write: for these words are true and faithful."

6 And he said unto me,

"IT IS DONE."

"I am Alpha and Omega,

the beginning and the end.

I will give unto him that is athirst of the fountain of the water of life freely.

7 **He that overcometh shall inherit all things; and I will be his God, and he shall be my son."**
8 "But the fearful, and unbelieving, and the abominable, and murderers, and whoremongers, and sorcerers, and idolaters, and all liars, shall have their part in the lake which burneth with fire and brimstone: which is the second death."

9 And there came unto me one of the seven angels which had the seven vials full of the seven last plagues, and talked with me, saying,

"Come hither,
I will shew thee the bride, the Lamb's wife."

10 And he carried me away in the spirit to a great and high mountain, and shewed me that great city, the holy Jerusalem, descending out of heaven from God,
11 Having the glory of God: and her light was like unto a stone most precious, even like a jasper stone, clear as crystal;
12 And had a wall great and high, and had **twelve gates**, and at the gates twelve angels, and names written thereon, which are **the names of the twelve tribes of the children of Israel**:
13
- on the east three gates;
- on the north three gates;
- on the south three gates; and
- on the west three gates.

14 And the wall of the city had **twelve foundations**, and in them the names of **the twelve apostles of the Lamb**.

15 And he that talked with me had a GOLDEN REED to measure the CITY, and the GATES thereof, and the WALL thereof.

16 And the CITY lieth **foursquare**, and the length is as large
as the breadth: and he measured the city with the reed,
twelve thousand furlongs. The length and the breadth and
the height of it are equal.

17 And he measured the WALL thereof, an hundred and forty
and four cubits, according to the measure of a man, that is,
of the angel.
18 And the building of the wall of it was of jasper: and the city
was pure gold, like unto clear glass.
19 And the foundations of the wall of the city were garnished
with all manner of precious stones.
- The first foundation was jasper;
- the second, sapphire;
- the third, a chalcedony;
- the fourth, an emerald;
20 - The fifth, sardonyx;
- the sixth, sardius;
- the seventh, chrysolite;
- the eighth, beryl;
- the ninth, a topaz;
- the tenth, a chrysoprasus;
- the eleventh, a jacinth;
- the twelfth, an amethyst.

21 And the twelve GATES were **twelve pearls**; every several
gate was of one pearl: and the STREET of the city was
pure gold, as it were transparent glass.

22 And I saw NO TEMPLE therein: for **the Lord God
Almighty and the Lamb are the temple of it.**

23 And the city had no need of the sun, neither of the moon, to
shine in it: for

**the glory of God did lighten it,
and the Lamb is the light thereof.**

24 And the nations of them which are saved shall walk in the
light of it: and the kings of the earth do bring their glory
and honour into it.
25 And the GATES of it shall not be shut at all by day: for
there shall be NO NIGHT there.
26 And they shall bring the glory and honour of the nations
into it.

27 **And there shall in no wise enter into it any thing that
defileth, neither whatsoever worketh abomination, or
maketh a lie: but they which are written in the
LAMB'S BOOK OF LIFE.**

Rev. 22

1 And he shewed me a
PURE RIVER OF WATER OF LIFE,
clear as crystal,
proceeding out of the throne of GOD and of the LAMB.

2 In the midst of the street of it, and on either side of the
river, was there the

TREE OF LIFE,

which bare twelve manner of fruits,
and
yielded her fruit every month:
and
the leaves of the tree were for the healing of the nations.

Vision 7

A New Heaven and a New Earth

Marriage of the Lamb—The Ascension

Rev. 21–Rev. 22:2

When Jesus was with us on earth, he promised there was a way for us to know God; that is, 'I,' Christ, would lead us to eternal harmony where our perceptions would be altered dramatically from hope and faith to God-present being. All prophecies are about to be fulfilled and to end, for they all point to the awareness of one event: the translation of man and the universe back to original Spirit, Mind, Love. We have been preparing for this moment—the end of time and the presence of *new*—and we are ready to celebrate the marriage of the Lamb and the Lamb's wife.

From their earth-based vantage point, Jesus' immediate disciples saw him separated from them and carried up into heaven. They could not follow because they were not sufficiently prepared. Sixty years later, John was prepared to share the event from the mount of vision. He had taken off his earthly weights, followed Jesus' preparatory instructions, put on his own white mental garment, and was freely accepted into the marriage.

Like John, we all must become spiritually prepared. First, we gain dominion over evil suggestion, which translates the body into dominion form—resurrection. Then, at the advent of ascension consciousness, the remnant memory of the whole so-called experience of this finite world vanishes, and New Jerusalem descends upon us—man rises to a new heaven and a new earth.

One might be tempted to think that since this vision is of the ascension (ascended consciousness), it must be unknowable until we ourselves leave earth permanently; however, this was not an intellectual exercise for John. Although it surpassed human understanding, this spiritual presence was available to him right there on Patmos;

otherwise, he would not have been able to share it with us. John's purpose was not to impress us with his attainment of this state of awareness, but it was to encourage us to proceed with our own demonstration. The beauty of this vision lies in our ability to master the ascension idea from right where we are on this plane of existence. Even in this world, all tears shall be wiped away, and there will be a cessation of sickness, sin, death, and hell.

1 **And I saw a new heaven and a new earth: for the first heaven and the first earth were passed away; and there was no more sea.**

New can mean the setting aside of one idea for the dawning of another, but new can also define the nature and character of an idea as pristine, virgin pure, clean, and so forth. This new consciousness and framework is, indeed, pristine and virgin pure, for the taint of old concepts of awareness has vanished. No more mortal thoughts remain—no birth and no death. The swirling sea of random mental energies no longer exists to our ascended consciousness. "Be still, and know that I am God" (Ps. 46:10) has become a reality.

2 **And I John saw the holy city, new Jerusalem, coming down from God out of heaven, prepared as a bride adorned for her husband.**

While standing in a glass elevator looking up, we may think the top of the building is coming down to us, but from the ground view, the elevator is ascending to a higher level. From the vantage point of Jesus' earthbound disciples, he ascended out of their sight, but Jesus saw his New Jerusalem coming down to him from the vantage point of the one ascending. John shared Jesus' view, was caught up with him, and saw his new-conscious home settle on him.

New Jerusalem is not a physical structure in any sense of the imagination. John found no better term to describe his vision for which there are no human words. Wholly spiritual realities do not translate to the earth-based mind, but when present in this new reality, man is preparing to be wed to his true-home consciousness. The man child is being caught up unto God and to his throne.

3 **And I heard a great voice out of heaven saying, Behold, the tabernacle of God is with men, and he will dwell with them, and they shall be his people, and God himself shall be with them, and be their God.**

All messages out of heaven are heard in heaven, for there is no satanic background noise to distract from the utterance of Truth. There is only one listener-responder: perfect man.

Before his crucifixion, Jesus identified the temple as his body that would be visibly rebuilt. Here, at the ascension, Jesus' angel is describing a tabernacle of God with men as cumulative body. "Where two or three are gathered together in my name" (Matt. 18:20) has become a tabernacle of infinite proportions: the gathering place for all God's children, the structure of one infinite God manifest as One. This vision is both inspirational and practical, for its purpose here on earth is to house the platform for the healing of nations. All the necessary prophecies are available to us and ready for us to understand and realize.

4 **And God shall wipe away all tears from their eyes; and there shall be no more death, neither sorrow, nor crying, neither shall there be any more pain: for the former things are passed away.**

All that was once contrary to God—which we called Satan, the devil, evil, the accuser, and the dragon that appeared as a phantasmagoric reality in the vacuity of ignorance—will assuredly disappear with the light of understanding. That which we greatly feared, and suffered as a consequence of that fear, has turned out to be a demonstrable illusion.

5 **And he that sat upon the throne said, Behold, I make all things new. And he said unto me, Write: for these words are true and faithful.**

The mortal concept of time has been swept away, and *this is now!* New cannot be added to or left behind and is, therefore, permanent. That which is inscribed in the newness of now is a kind of spiritual substance that pervades this higher consciousness.

6 **And he said unto me, It is done. I am Alpha and Omega, the beginning and the end. I will give unto him that is athirst of the fountain of the water of life freely.**

Alpha and Omega has neither beginning nor end: it includes within itself all history, prophecy, and fulfillment in the *now.* Divine Life animates all the living there is, and the Woman bringing forth the man child illustrates how Love feeds those who thirst for it.

7 **He that overcometh shall inherit all things; and I will be his God, and he shall be my son.**

Life, Truth, Love is manifest as one all-inclusive tabernacle body. As we realize this fact, we win our inheritance as sons and daughters of God and command the throne view.

8 **But the fearful, and unbelieving, and the abominable, and murderers, and whoremongers, and sorcerers, and idolaters, and all liars, shall have their part in the lake which burneth with fire and brimstone: which is the second death.**

Truth forever inflames a lie, and all who entertain falsehood must suffer the fatal stench of brimstone burning until there is no lie or liar left to be entertained. From heavenly consciousness, there is no recognition or attachment to satanic suggestion or belief because any thought that God does not think is impossible. Neither human birth nor death touches Mind's manifestation.

9 **And there came unto me one of the seven angels which had the seven vials full of the seven last plagues, and talked with me, saying, Come hither, I will shew thee the bride, the Lamb's wife.**

The same messenger that brought what we thought were curses come to plague us is also the one leading us to the bride. Divine Love understood is the Lamb's wife, which gives us the wisdom to profit from all the nuggets of purpose in every event of our lives.

On the day of Pentecost, everyone was filled with the Holy Ghost, spoke with other tongues, and understood the meaning universally. This Holy Ghost Comforter enables us to understand bridal chamber consciousness: "And nothing shall be impossible unto you" (Matt. 17:20). The angel is not speaking of some knowledge of salvation in the distant future, but of a present witnessing potential.

10–11 **And he carried me away in the spirit to a great and high mountain, and shewed me that great city, the holy Jerusalem, descending out of heaven from God, Having the glory of God: and her light was like unto a stone most precious, even like a jasper stone, clear as crystal;**

Spiritual expectancy is the only transport, and transfiguration is the only destination. Divine Mind, already infinite and universal, appears to expand as we approach the Love of being. Then love settles on us, surrounds us, and embraces us. When God is understood (transparent), there is no opacity of thought capable of receiving or casting shadows. Infinite good is crystal clear. Physically, crystal has no illuminating qualities of its own but reflects the light that passes through it. If that illumination shines through it from within, like the glow of a light bulb, it approximates the nature of all form ideas in ascended consciousness. Holy

Jerusalem is the presence of exalted consciousness where all these ideas reside.

12–13 **And had a wall great and high, and had twelve gates, and at the gates twelve angels, and names written thereon, which are the names of the twelve tribes of the children of Israel: On the east three gates; on the north three gates; on the south three gates; and on the west three gates.**

The exalted consciousness of Truth and Love is its own defense. The pattern on Aaron's breastplate with twelve stones arranged in four rows—three stones on each side—prophesied the ultimate salvation of the children of Israel. This prophecy is fulfilled in all men as the veil of ignorance is removed and replaced by the clear spectrum of the Mind of God. Each facing direction—eastward, northward, southward, and westward—indicates a progressive stage of awareness that when mastered, opens our mental portals to radiate divine light. It is upon this framework that we work out the problem of being. Each viewing direction involves three phases of development: first, we break from our ignorance and discover the existence of the primal element involved; second, this element is established in our thought as an abiding faith; and third, we demonstrate that element by many infallible proofs and ascend from faith to understanding. For John, all these elemental stages had been thoroughly mastered; otherwise, he would not have witnessed New Jerusalem.

Eastward: The star that was seen in the East pointed to the animated presentation of Christ in the man Jesus, where the idea of *God with us* could dawn on human consciousness.

Northward: The North Star fixed in the heavens represents the unmovable Word, which would have been unknowable without the Christ.

Southward: The Southern Cross in the sky requires us to do our part in following and repeating the Master's demonstration.

Westward: As the understanding from each of the previous elements is gained, the sky brightens until there is no darkness at all. Looking out from the star in the east, residing in the presence of the Word, and having proven the eternal nature of Life, we arrive home at the beginning and understand that these holy walls constitute the Only—one whole being.

These open gates radiating outward upon a perfect universe have had several earlier manifestations: Malachi assured the children of Israel that the "windows of heaven" would pour them out blessings from above; Rev. 4 described the nature of God with four beasts "full of eyes before and behind"; and Rev. 12 showed us "a Woman clothed with the sun," wearing a "crown of twelve stars." From the priesthood of Aaron's breastplate to the crown of stars worn by the Woman, the perfect man as all-seeing and all-knowing manifestation is king and priest unto God. John saw that the early symbols and allegories presented by Moses and the prophets were prophetic of this higher vision.

14 **And the wall of the city had twelve foundations, and in them the names of the twelve apostles of the Lamb.**

Moses could not explain ascended consciousness to his friends but intuitively read the divine pattern and illustrated it with a symbolic temple in the wilderness. It took the testimony and practice of the apostles to lay the living foundation for New Jerusalem.

Each experience in Christian practice builds one's faith and sets a living stone in one's foundation.

15 **And he that talked with me had a golden reed to measure the city, and the gates thereof, and the wall thereof.**

The angel with the golden pen must verify that every word recorded upon one's spiritual forehead and heart is identical to every Word that proceeds out of the mouth of God. As each divine impulse is validated by measurable proofs, we find it written in the Lamb's book of life.

> Who shall ascend into the hill of the Lord? or who shall stand in his holy place? He that hath clean hands, and a pure heart; who hath not lifted up his soul unto vanity, nor sworn deceitfully (Ps. 24:3–4).

16 **And the city lieth foursquare, and the length is as large as the breadth: and he measured the city with the reed, twelve thousand furlongs. The length and the breadth and the height of it are equal.**

The great city with four equal sides emphasizes the all-inclusive nature of this presence, as in the previous chapter where the passage describes "the four quarters of the earth"—meaning all the earth.

17 **And he measured the wall thereof, an hundred and forty and four cubits, according to the measure of a man, that is, of the angel.**

Humanly, a cubit was the length of the forearm, but an angel's forearm has nothing whatsoever to do with mortal body measurements since there is no translation from matter to Spirit. It is the extent of the Word understood that is measured in its fullness and verified completely (twelve times).

> I will redeem you with a stretched out arm (Exod. 6:6).

18 **And the building of the wall of it was of jasper: and the city was pure gold, like unto clear glass.**

Although Jasper is opaque and appears to have many different colors when contaminated by other elements, here it is transparent with no taint of earth.

> The stone which the builders rejected is become the head of the corner (Mark 12:10).

19–20 **And the foundations of the wall of the city were garnished with all manner of precious stones. The first foundation was jasper; the second, sapphire; the third, a chalcedony; the fourth, an emerald; The fifth, sardonyx; the sixth, sardius; the seventh, chrysolite; the eighth, beryl; the ninth, a topaz; the tenth, a chrysoprasus; the eleventh, a jacinth; the twelfth, an amethyst.**

Each of the stones represents the testimony of *God with us* as the way out of every type and condition of mortal mentality. Proofs of our fidelity are the foundation stones that ultimately allow us to stand on holy ground in the Promised Land—New Jerusalem.

The stones in the high priest's breastplate are prophetic of the gems that the twelve tribes of Israel become as they ascend the scale from bickering depravity to glorified sons and daughters. It is said that the last stone, Jasper, represented the house of Benjamin, Jacob's last son; yet it is the first foundation stone of the city of God: "The first shall be last; and the last first" (Mark 10:31). Love, the highest idea of God, is the first and most important to understand, but for man, it is the last to be demonstrated. The twelve apostles of the Lamb demonstrated the end from the beginning.

21 **And the twelve gates were twelve pearls; every several gate was of one pearl: and the street of the city was pure gold, as it were transparent glass.**

Each of Jacob's twelve sons had flawed personalities as varied as those of all mankind. We overcome our earthly connection by peeling away what human birth and mortal history has done to us, thus revealing the pearl of great price right there within. We each must discover this pearl of our being and stand porter at the open gates of the temple. Jacob was given his new identity, Israel, through this very process. Now John, having momentarily overcome his earthly connection, looked out upon the universe through the open gates of divine consciousness.

22 **And I saw no temple therein: for the Lord God Almighty and the Lamb are the temple of it.**

The full manifestation of Spirit no longer worships effect but is living infinite cause, not limited body. *God with us* is the conscious awareness of the structure and pattern of Truth and Love.

23 **And the city had no need of the sun, neither of the moon, to shine in it: for the glory of God did lighten it, and the Lamb is the light thereof.**

Spiritually enlightened consciousness is lit from within, having the Lamb of Love as its only source. There is no need or possibility of any external light. With boundless Love at the center, holy Jerusalem has no concept of *out* or *in*.

24 **And the nations of them which are saved shall walk in the light of it: and the kings of the earth do bring their glory and honour into it.**

Those who have gained the victory stand as light bearers full of glory and honor "like unto the Son of man."

25 **And the gates of it shall not be shut at all by day: for there shall be no night there.**

Residing in Holy Jerusalem consciousness, there are no closed doors because from the mount of vision, there are no doors at all. The shell in which we once hid ourselves for fear of the unknown has disappeared. There is no unknown, no darkness, no interruption, and no blocked connection with God.

26 **And they shall bring the glory and honour of the nations into it.**

All ideas support and praise one another as one universal, amen consciousness.

27 **And there shall in no wise enter into it any thing that defileth, neither whatsoever worketh abomination, or maketh a lie: but they which are written in the Lamb's book of life.**

Infinite good identifies and classifies itself, and there is no other good and no other self. "Thou shalt have no other gods before me" (Exod. 20:3) is literally fulfilled.

Rev. 22

1 **And he shewed me a pure river of water of life, clear as crystal, proceeding out of the throne of God and of the Lamb.**

The fountain of Life is the primal energy of infinite Mind, God. The Lamb—as manifestation, image, likeness, and Son of man—is the appearance of all that God is in the center as well as the circumference of being.

2 **In the midst of the street of it, and on either side of the river, was there the tree of life, which bare twelve manner of fruits, and yielded her fruit every month: and the leaves of the tree were for the healing of the nations.**

The tree of life is one of the first spiritual symbols recorded in the Bible, but it was inaccessible to a disobedient Adam and a foolish Eve. The journey back to that tree across the currents of evil appears difficult, but the divine solution is always at hand. Man's translation from sense to Soul has three phases: belief, faith, and understanding.

Belief: When Moses stood beside the Red Sea waiting for the parting of the water, the people were humbled by his courage. In the middle of the sea with a wall on each side, they were guided as a mother cares for her children. When they stood on the other shore, they believed that they had witnessed God with them, and so began their journey out of mental slavery.

Faith: Jesus stood on the shore of human wants and woes with all humanity behind him, waiting for the deep waters of human fear to part. With a sweet touch and penetrating eye, he cut through the illusions of the material senses and showed man his divine potential. He walked through the Red Sea of human events with us. The two-edged sword of Truth that he wielded, forever severed our connection to Adam's race. On the other side, he climbed ashore and directed our path upward, unencumbered by so-called laws of the flesh.

Christ, manifest in the flesh, brought us to the shore of the river of Life by delivering all manner of fruits (blessings) to waiting humanity. Jesus promised us that there was another shore where we would find the Promised Land, and that the 'I' (intelligence of God) would come to us as a Comforter to bring all things to our remembrance.

Understanding: The understanding of God that Jesus knew and demonstrated is the Comforter. The tree of Life never leaves the harmony of heaven for earth, and it never mingles with the soiled sea of mortal thoughts but continually draws all men from above like a spiritual beacon. This Comforter presence is attainable here and now, as it was for John. When we realize Life to be everywhere, we discover ourselves to be the fruit of Mind's universe as we were at the beginning.

While here on earth, we may be striving to solve the problem of being by working through dilemma after dilemma as we walk the thorn road that the Master trod; however, the very solution we seek is, and always has been, right in front of our faces. In our blindness, we thought the solution was on the other side of the river, but to the Comforter,

THERE IS NO PROBLEM OF BEING.

THE BEGINNING AND THE END

Rev. 22:3–21

3 (1) And there shall be no more curse:
(2) but the throne of God and of the Lamb shall be in it;
(3) and his servants shall serve him:
4 (4) And they shall see his face;
(5) and his name shall be in their foreheads.
5 (6) And there shall be no night there; and they need no candle, neither light of the sun;
(7) for the Lord God giveth them light: and they shall reign for ever and ever.

6 And he said unto me,
"These sayings are faithful and true: and the Lord God of the holy prophets sent his angel to shew unto his servants the things which must shortly be done."

7 **"Behold, I come quickly: blessed is he that keepeth the sayings of the prophecy of this book."**

8 And I John saw these things, and heard them. And when I
had heard and seen, I fell down to worship before the feet
of the angel which shewed me these things.
9 Then saith he unto me, "See thou do it not: for I am thy
fellowservant, and of thy brethren the prophets, and of
them which keep the sayings of this book: **worship God**."

10 And he saith unto me, **"Seal not the sayings of the prophecy of this book: for the time is at hand.**

11 He that is unjust, let him be unjust still: and he which is
filthy, let him be filthy still: and he that is righteous, let him
be righteous still: and he that is holy, let him be holy still.
12 And, behold, I come quickly; and my reward is with me, to
give every man according as his work shall be."

13 **"I am**
Alpha and Omega,
THE BEGINNING AND THE END,
the first and the last."

14 "Blessed are they that do his commandments, that they may
have right to the TREE OF LIFE, and may enter in through
the gates into the city.
15 For without are dogs, and sorcerers, and whoremongers,
and murderers, and idolaters, and whosoever loveth and
maketh a lie."

16 I Jesus have sent mine angel to testify unto you these things
in the churches.
"I am the root and the offspring of David, and
the bright and morning star."

17 And the SPIRIT and the BRIDE say, *"Come."*
And let him that heareth say, *"Come."*
And let him that is athirst come.
And whosoever will, let him take the WATER OF LIFE
freely.
18 For I testify unto every man that heareth the words of the
prophecy of this book, If any man shall add unto these
things, God shall add unto him the plagues that are written
in this book:
19 And if any man shall take away from the words of the book
of this prophecy, God shall take away his part out of the
book of life, and out of the holy city, and from the things
which are written in this book.

20 He which testifieth these things saith, "Surely I come
quickly."

"Amen. Even so, come, Lord Jesus."

21 The grace of our Lord Jesus Christ be with you all.
"Amen."

The Beginning and the End

Rev. 22:3–21
If we have been listening with ears to hear, we should now understand the meaning of Jesus' profound statements.

> I can of mine own self do nothing (John 5:30).
>
> Which of you convinceth me of sin? (John 8:46).
>
> I have meat to eat that ye know not of (John 4:32).
>
> No man hath ascended up to heaven, but he that came down from heaven, even the Son of man which is in heaven (John 3:13).
>
> I am the living bread which came down from heaven: if any man eat of this bread, he shall live for ever: and the bread that I will give is my flesh, which I will give for the life of the world (John 6:51).
>
> Ye shall know the truth, and the truth shall make you free (John 8:32).
>
> Be of good cheer; I have overcome the world (John 16:33).

As the Comforter that we so dearly sought descends upon us, we fulfill another of Jesus' prophecies.

> Verily, verily, I say unto you, He that believeth on me, the works that I do shall he do also; and greater works than these shall he do; because I go unto my Father (John 14:12).

The entire book of Revelation is the prophecy and fulfillment of man as Jesus' angel presented it to us.

Summary of the 7 Visions

3–5 **And there shall be no more curse: but the throne of God and of the Lamb shall be in it; and his servants shall serve him: And they shall see his face; and his name shall be in their foreheads. And there shall be no night there; and they need no candle, neither light of the sun; for the Lord God giveth them light: and they shall reign for ever and ever.**

The veil has been lifted. This brief summary touches on all the lessons of the seven visions of Revelation:

1. "There shall be no more curse" reminds us that the great whore and Babylon will lose all sense of reality (Rev. 13–17).
2. "The throne of God and of the Lamb" is defined (Rev. 4–5).
3. As the Lamb breaks the seven seals of the book, we learn how it is that "his servants shall serve him" (Rev. 6–8:1).
4. The baptism by fire, a LITTLE BOOK OPEN, and a REED LIKE UNTO ROD enable us to hear the sounding of the seventh trumpet and "see his face" (Rev. 8–11).
5. As we witness the Woman clothed with the sun, bearing the man child caught up unto God and to his throne, we understand how it is that "his name shall be in their foreheads" (Rev. 12).
6. In resurrection consciousness, John sees that "there shall be no night there; and they need no candle, neither light of the sun; for the Lord God giveth them light" (Rev. 19–20).
7. In ascension consciousness, "they shall reign for ever and ever" (Rev. 21–22:2).

Introduction Key—Binding the End to the Beginning

6 **And he said unto me, These sayings are faithful and true: and the Lord God of the holy prophets sent his angel to shew unto his servants the things which must shortly be done.**

The Revelation of Jesus Christ, which God gave unto him, to shew unto his servants things which must shortly come to pass (Rev. 1:1).

Beginning and Ending Message—Restating the Seven Messages to the Seven Churches

7 **Behold, I come quickly: blessed is he that keepeth the sayings of the prophecy of this book.**

(1st) The church in Ephesus is warned not to lose the original inspiration: "Thou hast left thy first love. . . . repent, and do the first works."

Those who never lose sight of their spiritual essence move quickly from prophecy to fulfillment, undisturbed by the grand lessons during the intervening years.

8–9 **And I John saw these things, and heard them. And when I had heard and seen, I fell down to worship before the feet of the angel which shewed me these things. Then saith he unto me, See thou do it not: for I am thy fellowservant, and of thy brethren the prophets, and of them which keep the sayings of this book: worship God.**

(2nd) "The first and the last, which was dead, and is alive" said to the church in Smyrna, "Be thou faithful unto death, and I will give thee a crown of life."

Even a temporary belief in a power other than God misdirects worship. Christ's angel messenger always points us in the right direction and keeps pointing until Life's promise reigns in us.

10–12 **And he saith unto me, Seal not the sayings of the prophecy of this book: for the time is at hand. He that is unjust, let him be unjust still: and he which is filthy, let him be filthy still: and he that is righteous, let him be righteous still: and he that is holy, let him be holy still. And, behold, I come quickly; and my reward is with me, to give every man according as his work shall be.**

(3rd) The sword with two edges taught the receptive in Pergamos to make clear distinctions between the thoughts and actions that "cast a stumbling block" and the proper ideas and activity of Christ. The Nicolaitans taught holiness from the sinner's perspective, thereby attempting to mix Spirit and Satan.

Spiritual clarity and holy practice is of the utmost importance when deciphering scripture: "Be instant in season, out of season" (2 Tim. 4:2).

13–15 **I am Alpha and Omega, the beginning and the end, the first and the last. Blessed are they that do his commandments, that they may have right to the tree of life, and may enter in through the gates into the city. For without are dogs, and sorcerers, and whoremongers, and murderers, and idolaters, and whosoever loveth and maketh a lie.**

(4th) "The Son of God" with "eyes like unto a flame of fire" said to Thyatira, "I will give unto every one of you according to your works." The seduction and fornication of Jezebel caused great tribulation. "I am he which searcheth the reins and hearts: . . . hold fast till I come."

All-encompassing good is Life experienced. Faithfully following the letter and spirit of the Commandments is your perfect guide to eternal life. You have all the tools you need. An impure thought—a speck of imperfection—is enough to deny your inheritance.

16 **I Jesus have sent mine angel to testify unto you these things in the churches. I am the root and the offspring of David, and the bright and morning star.**

(5th) "He that hath the seven Spirits of God, and the seven stars" said to Sardis, "Be watchful, and strengthen the things which remain, that are ready to die."

According to the historical record, the time between prophecy and fulfillment was often thousands of years, but when we watch with conviction, we see how "the root and the offspring" arrive together as one dawning star message and messenger. When we devote ourselves to the understanding of spiritual cause, we discover the Christ man to be enlightened effect. Revelation knits the end to the beginning in one grand sphere.

17 **And the Spirit and the bride say, Come. And let him that heareth say, Come. And let him that is athirst come. And whosoever will, let him take the water of life freely.**

(6th) "He that is holy, he that is true, he that hath the key of David, he that openeth, and no man shutteth; and shutteth, and no man openeth" said, "Behold, I have set before thee an open door, . . . know that I have loved thee."

Philadelphia held the key to the water of Life. It is Love that is calling us, drawing us to the wedding, opening the windows of heaven, and rolling away the stones of mortality, sin, and death. He who begins with divine Love has already found the water of Life.

18 **For I testify unto every man that heareth the words of the prophecy of this book, If any man shall add unto these things, God shall add unto him the plagues that are written in this book:**

(7th) "The Amen, the faithful and true witness, the beginning of the creation of God" said to the Laodiceans that "because thou art lukewarm, and neither cold nor hot, I will spue thee out of my mouth. Because thou sayest, I am rich, and increased with goods . . ."

Why is the attempt to add something to this prophecy judged so harshly? Having the words or intellectual sense of the Comforter and trying to use that intellect to share one's feeble sense of God with humanity is a crime against Christ's method. Disastrous effects will follow, for the sword of Truth guards the gate against the lukewarm helper who unwittingly tries to teach the knowledge of God. It is difficult enough for searching humanity to find and follow the true path, but it becomes more difficult when someone attempts to lead without being called and mislabels that path, claiming to be a holy one and offering to sell the answers that man is seeking without having the unction of Love. This man must lose *his* way through suffering until Truth is realized. The Spirit that is Love speaks for itself, draws from above, is already whole and complete, and is the only teacher.

19 **And if any man shall take away from the words of the book of this prophecy, God shall take away his part out of the book of life, and out of the holy city, and from the things which are written in this book.**

Any attempt to deprive man the freedom and opportunity to work out the problem of being, by taking away his spiritual tools, denies man's ready access to the solutions God has presented. Consciously fighting against God is the fastest way to the lake that burns with fire and brimstone, for there is no personal guilt greater than that which one receives for denying the existence of *good*. Without *good*, what can one expect? To willfully hide the fulfillment of prophecy is to commit suicide, follow Judas' path, and miss life entirely.

Benediction

20 **He which testifieth these things saith, Surely I come quickly. Amen. Even so, come, Lord Jesus.**

The moment you understand this unveiling, you will know from whence 'I' came, and you will know Me.

21 **The grace of our Lord Jesus Christ be with you all. Amen.**

Seven rewards of grace were offered to the seven churches:

1. To him that overcometh will I give to eat of the tree of life, which is in the midst of the paradise of God (Rev. 2:7).

2. He that overcometh shall not be hurt of the second death (Rev. 2:11).

3. To him that overcometh will I give to eat of the hidden manna, and will give him a white stone, and in the stone a new name written, which no man knoweth saving he that receiveth it (Rev. 2:17).

4. And he that overcometh, and keepeth my works unto the end, to him will I give power over the nations: And he shall rule them with a rod of iron; as the vessels of a potter shall they be broken to shivers: even as I received of my Father. And I will give him the morning star (Rev. 2:26–28).

5. He that overcometh, the same shall be clothed in white raiment; and I will not blot out his name out of the book of life, but I will confess his name before my Father, and before his angels (Rev. 3:5).

6. Him that overcometh will I make a pillar in the temple of my God, and he shall go no more out: and I will write upon him the name of my God, and the name of the city of my God, which is new Jerusalem, which cometh down out of heaven from my God: and I will write upon him my new name (Rev. 3:12).

7. To him that overcometh will I grant to sit with me in my throne, even as I also overcame, and am set down with my Father in his throne (Rev. 3:21).

Seven times Jesus' angel urged us…

"He that hath an ear, let him hear what the Spirit saith unto the churches."
"He that hath an ear, let him hear what the Spirit saith unto the churches."
"He that hath an ear, let him hear what the Spirit saith unto the churches."
"He that hath an ear, let him hear what the Spirit saith unto the churches."
"He that hath an ear, let him hear what the Spirit saith unto the churches."
"He that hath an ear, let him hear what the Spirit saith unto the churches."
"He that hath an ear, let him hear what the Spirit saith unto the churches."

Grace never left.

Amen.